# American Politics and Media

Film im Englischunterricht

# American Politics and Media

## Wag the Dog
## Swing Vote
## The War Room

Unterrichtshinweise und Kopiervorlagen
von Frauke Vieregge

Ernst Klett Sprachen
Stuttgart

Film im Englischunterricht

# American Politics and Media

## Wag the Dog
## Swing Vote
## The War Room

von Frauke Vieregge

In diesem Werk werden die Begriffe „Schülerinnen und Schüler" und „Lehrerinnen und Lehrer" durch „SuS" und „LuL" ersetzt, um einen flüssigen Lesestil zu gewährleisten.

**Bildcredits:**

S. 66 o. li. © shutterstock (Alan Freed), New York
S. 66 o. re. © shutterstock, New York
S. 66 m. li. © Corbis (Brooks Kraft), Düsseldorf
S. 66 m. re. © Picture-Alliance, Frankfurt
S. 66 u. li. © Getty Images (Cynthia Johnson/Time Life Pictures), München
S. 69 © shutterstock (Kami Gami), New York
S. 74 Christian Dekelver, Weinstadt
S. 81 © shutterstock (Alan Freed), New York
S. 84 © Cinetext GmbH (Richter), Frankfurt
S. 100 © Action Press GmbH (REX FEATURES), Hamburg



1. Auflage 1 5 4 3 2 1 | 2014 13 12 11 10

Alle Drucke dieser Auflage sind unverändert und können im Unterricht nebeneinander verwendet werden.

Internetadresse: www.klett.de / www.lektueren.com

Autorin: Frauke Vieregge

Redaktion: Rona McGeoch
Layoutkonzeption: Elmar Feuerbach
Gestaltung und Satz: Satz & mehr, Besigheim
Umschlaggestaltung: Elmar Feuerbach
Titelbild: Shutterstock images/Junker, New York
Druck und Bindung: AZ Druck und Datentechnik GmbH, Heisinger Straße 16, 87437 Kempten/Allgäu
Printed in Germany

ISBN 978-3-12-577467-4

9 783125 774674

# Inhaltsverzeichnis

# Vorwort / Didaktisch-methodische Anmerkungen

Alle 4 Jahre werden wir vor die Wahl gestellt, wer unser Land regieren soll. Es werden Plakate aufgestellt, Wahlkampfveranstaltungen in Fußgängerzonen und großen Hallen abgehalten, einige Kandidaten stellen sich den unsicheren Bürgern direkt oder rufen diese sogar zu Hause an, um Stimme zu werben. Die Wahlkampfmaschinerie bleibt dem Normalbürger verschlossen. Niemand weiß, wie viel Geld die Kampagnen der einzelnen Kandidaten die Parteien und den Staat kosten oder wie viele Menschen im Hintergrund für die einzelnen Kandidaten arbeiten. Die Parteien geben sich alle Mühe, am Tag nach der Wahl ist aber alles wieder vergessen, die Sieger triumphieren und relativieren meistens die von ihnen gemachten Wahlkampfversprechen, während die Verlierer behaupten, hervorragende Oppositionsarbeit zu leisten und ihre Wahlkampfziele so doch noch durchzusetzen.

Im Englischunterricht dürfen landeskundliche Themen nicht fehlen. Die Thematisierung des Medieneinflusses auf den US-amerikanischen Wahlkampf deckt nicht nur landeskundliche, sondern auch politische Themen ab und bietet gleichzeitig viele Möglichkeiten für eine kreative und interessante Gestaltung des Unterrichts. Neben der Vermittlung von Wissen über das US-amerikanische Wahlsystem, lässt sich im Verlauf dieser Unterrichtsreihe mit drei Filmen arbeiten, um das erlernte Wissen zu vertiefen und anzuwenden. Ein Vergleich mit dem deutschen Wahlsystem und der deutschen Wahlkampfmaschinerie findet statt, um den SuS Unterschiede aufzuzeigen und somit das interkulturelle Verständnis bzw. einen Transfer zu ermöglichen.

Die ausgewählten Filme *Wag the Dog, Swing Vote* und *The War Room* sind grundverschieden, ihre Kombination für diese Unterrichtsreihe jedoch sinnvoll, da sie den US-amerikanischen Wahlkampf aus verschiedenen Perspektiven beleuchten: *Wag the Dog* aus der Sicht des Beraterstabes des US-Präsidenten, *Swing Vote* aus der Sicht eines Wählers und *The War Room* als Dokumentarfilm. Die SuS können aufgrund ihres theoretischen Vorwissens die Filme nicht nur inhaltlich analysieren, sondern durch die Vermittlung von Aufnahmetechniken und Filmsprache auch die künstlerische Wirkung auf den Zuschauer. So werden die SuS kritischen Zuschauern und auch zu kritischen Wählern, die nicht mehr so leicht durch die „wunderbare Welt" der Medien zu beeinflussen sind.

Die SuS erarbeiten die Module 1-4 der Unterrichtseinheit mit Hilfe von verschiedenen Methoden und Arbeitsformen. Partner- bzw. Gruppenarbeitsphasen finden immer dann statt, wenn ein großer Umfang von Informationen zu bewältigen ist. Die Methode der Präsentation wird hier nicht nur als Möglichkeit eingesetzt, um einzelnen SuS eine Zusatzleistung anzubieten. Vielmehr sollen die SuS die Methode beherrschen lernen, um sie auch in anderen Fächern und außerhalb der Schule anwenden zu können.

# Modules

# Module I American Politics and Media

## Lernziele

- die SuS lernen das US-amerikanische Wahlsystem und die Art und Weise, wie der US-amerikanische Präsident gewählt wird, kennen
- die SuS erweitern ihr Wissen über die im Wahlkampf eingesetzten audio-visuellen Medien und deren Wirkung auf den Wähler
- die SuS erlernen die Analyse von audio-visuellen Medien durch Kenntnis der Fachtermini aus der Filmsprache
- die SuS wenden die erlernten Fachtermini zur Analyse von Spielfilmen und einem Dokumentarfilm an
- die SuS wenden ihr Hintergrundwissen über den US-amerikanischen Wahlkampf in handlungs- und produktionsorientierten Phasen zur Vorbereitung einer Präsentation an
- durch die umfangreiche Filmanalyse mit Verknüpfung des theoretischen Wissens werden die SuS zu kritischen Zuschauern und erkennen die manipulative Wirkung der audio-visuellen Medien in der Politik
- die SuS lernen die Methoden der Partner (PW)- und Gruppenarbeit (GW) zu beherrschen und damit unterschiedlichen Materialien zu bearbeiten

## Worksheets

### Worksheet 1: American Politics: Basic Information

#### Didaktische Anmerkungen
Die erste Stunde der Unterrichtsreihe beginnt mit einem stummen Impuls. Fotos der Kandidaten des Wahlkampfes 2008 ((ggfs. anpassen)) in den USA werden per Tageslichtprojektor den SuS präsentiert. Die SuS äußern sich spontan über die Kandidaten (Biographie, Wahlversprechen, besondere Ereignisse etc.). Die Ergebnisse werden an der Tafel festgehalten oder auf dem OHP in Tabellenform. Zu jedem Politiker soll ein prägnantes Ereignis gefunden werden, welches unverwechselbar mit ihm in Beziehung steht. Denkbar wären folgende Ereignisse: Obama: Friedensnobelpreis, John M^c Cain: Kriegsgefangenschaft im Vietnamkrieg; George W. Bush: umstrittenes Wahlergebnis 2004, Irakkrieg; Bill Clinton: Monika Lewinsky Affäre; Al Gore: Klimaschützer, Film „Eine unbequeme Wahrheit" über Klimawandel, JFK: Tod in Dallas, Kubakrise.

#### Aufgaben
**1** (Lead in) *What do you know about the American electoral system?*

**2** *Who are these candidates? What do you know about them and what they stand / stood for?*

#### Lösungen
individuelle Lösungen

## Worksheet 2: Glossary of Political Terms

### Didaktische Anmerkungen

Im Anschluss an diese freie Phase wird die Wissensbasis vorbereitet. Die SuS erhalten zunächst ein Infoblatt mit einem Glossar von themenspezifischem Vokabular, um den Wortschatz für die folgenden Stunden zu erarbeiten (diese kann im Laufe des Unterrichts ergänzt werden). Danach erfolgt eine Bearbeitung der Parteiprogramme von *Democrats* und *Republicans*.

## Worksheet 3: Elephant and Donkey: The Political Parties

### Didaktische Anmerkungen

In den USA gibt es zwei große Parteien, die *Republicans* und die *Democrats*, zwischen denen die Präsidentschaftswahl entschieden wird. Beide Parteien werden von Einzelpersonen und Institutionen unterstützt und die Mitglieder beider Parteien besetzen alle wichtigen Ämter in der nationalen, einzelstaatlichen und lokalen Regierung.

Die Texte sollen ein Einstieg in das Thema sein und die Wissensbasis für die spätere Erarbeitung der Kandidatenprofile liefern. Zunächst werden die Unterschiede zwischen den Parteien erarbeitet und dann ein kurzer Vergleich zu entsprechenden Parteien in Deutschland gezogen, um den SuS das Verständnis zu erleichtern. Anschließend sollen die SuS sich in der Hausaufgabe intensiver mit den Parteiprogrammen auseinandersetzen. Aus der gekürzten Fassung des Parteiprogramms soll ein Aspekt ausgewählt und mit Hilfe der Website der Partei und der Seite von CNN *http://edition.cnn.com/ELECTION/2008/issues/index.html* genauer erarbeitet werden (Auf der Seite der *Republicans* unter *„Issues“*, auf der der *Democrats* unter *„Agenda“*, von allen Aspekten existieren „druckerfreundliche“ Versionen). Die SuS schreiben ihre Ergebnisse auf Moderations- oder Karteikarten, die in der anschließenden Stunde an die Tafel geheftet werden. So findet ein Vergleich der Standpunkte der Parteien zum gleichen Thema statt.

### Aufgaben

1 *List the main differences between the two parties.*

2 *Find corresponding parties in Germany and compare the parties' programs.*

3 *Choose an issue from the excerpt you are interested in and find out more details on the parties' websites or the summary of issues on* http://edition.cnn.com/ELECTION/2008/issues/index.html

**Lösungen**

**1**

| **Republican Party** | **Democratic Party** |
|---|---|
| • free enterprise system is the most effective engine of economic progress, government should have no influence<br>• cut government spending and reduce government waste<br>• put the welfare system into the hands of organizations to minimize government costs<br>• no emission control of business by the government<br>• strong national defense, America must be ready to fight terrorism abroad in order to prevent it at home<br>• voters come from rural areas with a rather "traditional" standard of living | • government regulation and control of economic activity through taxes can better distribute wealth and services to the American people.<br>• keep the welfare system in government hands so that everyone is taken care of<br>• in the interest of the environment, oil companies should not be supported<br>• reduction of money spent on the military; protecting security should involve negotiations with other nations before resorting to aggressive actions<br>• "modern" and younger voters from urban areas |
| It is important to clarify the differences concerning certain aspects such as "environment". While the Democrats include the protection of the environment into their program (e.g. detailed information about biofuels), this aspect is missing in the Republican's program. | |

**2**

| **CDU/CSU** | **SPD** |
|---|---|
| • free enterprise system is the most effective engine of economic progress, government should have no influence, people can handle business and private life without the help of the government<br>• support of families with an emphasis on the middle class<br>• protection of environment not as important as flourishing business<br>• support of farmers/ rural areas<br>• voters come from rural areas with a rather "traditional" standard of living | • fair world order under government control to ensure that everyone who is disadvantaged is helped and taken care of<br>• equal opportunities for men and women<br>• business must be controlled by the state to prevent abuse of government money<br>• development of domestic renewable energy sources must be strengthened<br>• "modern" and younger voters from urban areas |

**3**

individuelle Lösungen

## Worksheet 4: How to Become President

### Didaktische Anmerkungen

Dieses Material dient zur Hintergrundinformation der SuS. Sie erlangen das notwendige Wissen über das Wahlsystem der USA, das sich sehr von dem deutschen Wahlsystem unterscheidet.

### Aufgaben

*Compare this to the electoral system in Germany and discuss the advantages and disadvantages of each system.*

**Lösungen**

| German Electoral System | US-American Electoral System |
|---|---|
| **Principles of Democratic Elections as Based on Art. 38 (2) of the German Constitution**<br>• universal: each citizen of at least 18 years of age is allowed to vote<br>• direct: the candidates are elected directly and not through members of an election meeting<br>• free: citizens cannot be forced to vote, no one is allowed to dictate the choice of party or candidate<br>• equal: each vote has the same weight, from income or prestige do not have an effect on the number of electoral votes<br>• secret: the secrecy of the ballot must be guaranteed | **Principle of Elections**<br>• anyone who is 18 years of age is allowed to vote<br>• there is no national list of eligible voters as in Germany, so citizens must register to vote<br>• the place of registration is the place where voters live; if they move they have to register again<br>• principles of universal, free, equal and secret right to vote as in Germany |
| **Electoral System**<br>• each citizen has two votes<br>• mixture of majority vote system and system of proportional representation to combine the advantages of those two electoral systems<br>• one vote for the direct election of a local candidate<br>• one vote for the political party, which makes lists of candidates<br>• seats in the parliament related to the number of votes each party gets in relation to the complete number of votes (e.g. 30% of votes = 30 seats if the parliament consists of 100 seats)<br>• party with the most votes elects *Bundeskanzler* who normally is the top candidate of the party<br>• *Bundespräsident* inaugurates *Bundeskanzler* | **Electoral System**<br>• two party system (every president since 1852 has been either a Republican or a Democrat)<br>• „single-member district system" applies. The candidate who gets elected is the one who gets the highest number of votes in their respective state.<br>• Presidents are elected indirectly, the voters are really voting for electors in each state<br>• in all states, the candidate who wins a plurality, receives all of that state's electoral votes.<br>• to win the presidential election, a candidate must earn an absolute majority at least 270 of the 538 electoral votes cast nationwide<br>• the President will be inaugurated on January 20 in the year after the election. From this time he is in office. |
| **Advantages**<br>• party representation mirrors support for party across the country<br>• provides voters with greater choice<br>• mid-term vacancies can be filled by next candidate down in list without holding another election<br>• share of seats won by a party in a constituency is compared with proportion of vote overall and discrepancies are corrected by allocation of seats from regional party lists. However, parties need to cross a 'threshold', e.g. 3 constituency seats or 5% of party vote.<br>• retain best features of plurality and majority systems – constituency based representation, parties are allocated seats more fairly | **Advantages**<br>• in this voting system the single winner is the person with the most votes; there is no requirement that the winner gain an absolute majority of votes<br>• preservation of the „one person, one vote" principle, wherein each voter is only able to cast one vote in a given election, where that vote can only go to one candidate. Plurality voting systems elect the candidate who is preferred first by the largest number of voters.<br>• plurality voting tends to promote two-party systems Supporters view this as beneficial, as parliamentary governments, or other coalitions, are typically more stable in two-party systems, and thus small minorities are not given undue voice. First-past-the-post minimizes the influence of third parties and thus arguably keeps out extremists. |

| Disadvantages | Disadvantages |
|---|---|
| • links between MP and constituencies are weaker because constituencies are multi-member<br>• less accountability to electors as a consequence<br>• lists are drawn up by parties, voters have very little choice<br>• creates 2 types of representatives – elected candidates and those appointed from regional lists<br>• creates larger constituencies than under current system | • voters come under pressure to vote for one of the two candidates they predict are most likely to win, even if their true preference is neither, because a vote for any other candidate will be likely to be wasted and have no impact on the final result<br>• as fewer choices are offered to the voters, voters may vote for a candidate with whom they largely disagree so as to oppose a candidate with whom they disagree even more<br>• one-party rule is more likely to lead to radical changes in government policy that are only favoured by a plurality or bare majority of the voters, whereas multi-party systems usually require greater consensus in order to make dramatic changes |

## Worksheet 5: An Election Quiz

### Didaktische Anmerkungen
Das Quiz rundet die theoretische Einheit ab und überprüft spielerische das Wissen der SuS.

### Aufgaben
*Fill in the blanks.*

### Lösungen
**1** four **2** thirty-five **3** Hillary Clinton, Barack Obama **4** John McCain **5** campaign **6** speeches, hands, **7** conventions **8** debates **9** November **10** swing **11** January 20, inauguration **12** White House

## Worksheet 6 : The Manipulative Media : Analysis of Photos

### Didaktische Ankmerkungen
Die SuS beschäftigen sich mit einer Auswahl von Fotos von Präsidentschaftskandidaten bzw. Präsidenten der USA und analysieren mit Hilfe des Arbeitsblattes ihre Wirkung.

### Aufgaben
*Analyse one photo of one of the presidential candidates / presidents of your choice following the method above.*

### Lösungen
Die Ergebnisse werden im Plenum vorgestellt und zur Diskussion gestellt; das entsprechende Foto sollte dann für die gesamte Klasse sichtbar sein (evtl. auf Folie ziehen). Der individuelle Aspekt der Analyse von Bildmedien muss im Vordergrund stehen, es gibt also keine richtigen oder falschen Antworten, was für die Diskussion im Plenum jedoch eine belebende Wirkung haben kann.

## Worksheet 7: Overview of Film Terminology

### Didaktische Anmerkungen

Diese Kopiervorlagen erläutern zentrale Aspekte der Filmanalyse. Den SuS sollen diese als Hilfe bei der Filmanalyse dienen. Es werden beispielsweise die Verwendung von Kameraeinstellung, Kamerawinkeln und Bildausschnitten erläutert.

## Worksheet 8: Analysis of Campaign Ads (Videos)

### Didaktische Anmerkungen

Als Einstieg sollten die SuS Gelegenheit bekommen sich einige Videos auf *www.c-span.org/politics* der *YouTube* erst einmal nur anzuschauen, bevor sie sich intensiver mit diesem Medium beschäftigen. Die Arbeitsblätter können auch schon in dieser Phase ausgeteilt und dann die unterschiedlichen Videos im Plenum besprochen werden, eine freie und „unverkrampfte" Herangehensweise an dieses für die SuS vielleicht noch unbekannte Medium ist aber zu befürworten, da nicht nur Bilder erfasst, sondern auch der Kommentar verstanden werden muss. Die SuS sollten dann mit Unterstützung der Arbeitsblätter Wahlkampfvideos der Kandidaten zu ein und demselben Thema vergleichen.

An dieser Stelle bietet es sich an einen Blick auf den täglichen Blog von Angela Merkel zu werfen. Die Bundeskanzlerin berichtet täglich in kurzen Videobotschaften über die neuesten politischen Ereignisse und Entscheidungen der Bundesregierung. Man könnte diese kurzen Filme – auch als Präsentationsleistung einzelner SuS – auf ihre wahlkampfpolitische Wirkung untersuchen und mit Videos der Oppositionsparteien vergleichen.

Angela Merkel: *http://www.bundeskanzlerin.de/Webs/BK/De/Mediathek/Videos/videos.html*

SPD: *http://www.youtube.com/spdvision*

FDP, CDU und Die Grünen sind auch bei YouTube mit eigenen Formaten vertreten, die FDP mit dem FDP Channel, die CDU mit CDU TV und die Grünen mit Kanal Grün

### Aufgaben

*Choose a candidate and then choose a campaign video and watch it in your group. Take notes.*

### Lösungen

There is an immense variety of video ads to be found on the Internet. The students should watch a TV ad because those are sure to reach the majority of the voters. The students should realize that the videos are always supported by music and that there is always a mixture of text and pictures. The most popular style to show the candidates is either during a campaign speech or in an interview; the interview is not a dialogue but the candidate's monologue about his/her issues. Then there are videos that don't include the candidate at all but where people talk about the candidate and state why they will vote for him or her (testimonials). The majority of the videos are presented by male speakers, the Obama videos hardly have any comment at all but use the text to ask rhetorical questions or comment on the pictures. When the opponent is attacked in the videos there hardly is any spoken but printed comment.

The sentence "I am ... and I approve this message." can be heard at the end of every video but that is about all they have in common. As mentioned the students should compare videos on the same issue to analyse how differently the candidates' campaign ads are.

## Worksheet 9: The Presidential Debates: Structure of a Debate

### Didaktische Anmerkungen

Bislang haben die SuS mit Texten und Internetseiten in Partner- und Gruppenarbeit gearbeitet. Bei der Erarbeitung eines der wichtigsten Pfeiler des US-amerikanischen Wahlkampfes, der *Presidential Debate*, kann nun handlungsorientiert und aktiv gearbeitet werden: mit einem Rollenspiel. Zunächst werden den SuS die Regeln der Debatte auf einem Arbeitsblatt zur Verfügung gestellt, damit sie die Debatte so realistisch wie möglich nachspielen können.

Die Anleitung zum Führen einer Debatte wird an die SuS-gruppen ausgeteilt. Den SuS wird nun Zeit zum Vorbereiten ihrer Rolle als Kandidat und Moderator gegeben. Die Gruppen sollten nicht größer als 5 Personen sein, die Gruppe, die die Rolle des Moderators vorbereitet, sollte aus 3 SuS bestehen.

Zur Vorbreitung kann eine Debatte aus dem Jahr 2004 angesehen werden. Dazu wird Zugang zum Internet benötigt, da die Debatten von C-Span als Realplayer-Datei angeboten wird (z. B. unter *http://www.case.edu/news/2004/9-04/tv_debates.htm*), aber nicht abgespeichert werden kann. Es werden von C-Span auch Tipps für die Zuschauer angeboten, die man den SuS als Arbeitsblatt aushändigen kann. So wird aus dem Anschauen der Debatte eine Hörverstehensübung.

### Aufgaben

*You are about to prepare a role play staging a Presidential Debate. You will choose a candidate and prepare his or her character with the help of worksheets and role cards. First, read the rules for a debate.*

## Worksheet 10: The Presidential Debates: Roleplay Cards

### Didaktische Anmerkungen

Das Rollenspiel sollte natürlich nicht die gleiche Länge haben wie eine reale Debatte. Es wird ein Zeitraum von 25 Minuten vorgeschlagen; das lässt ausreichend Zeit zur anschließenden Diskussion. Die SuS sollten in der Vorbereitung der Debatte ausreichend Zeit erhalten, ihre Rolle zu erschaffen.

### Aufgaben

*Imagine you are a candidate for president or the moderator at the debates. Prepare and carry out a debate.*

### Lösungen

The debate is going to be unique and the result cannot be foretold. There should be a lively discussion of campaign issues where the students can use their language skills and background knowledge about the candidates. The students know what a debate should look like and shouldn't have any problems creating their own debate. After the debate there should be a discussion about the result of the debate, how the students felt in their roles and what the audience thought of the debate. For homework, each student should write a review about the debate, so the audience has to take notes and the candidates and the moderator can use the notes they took during the debate.

## Worksheet 11: The Speeches: Barack Obama, New Hampshire, Jan 8, 2008

### Didaktische Anmerkungen

Barack Obama hielt diese Rede am 08.01.2008 nach den *Primaries* in New Hampshire und nachdem feststand, dass Hillary Clinton den Staat New Hampshire gewonnen hatte. Der *New Hampshire Primary* ist seit 1920 immer der erste der amerikanischen Präsidentschaftswahlen. Gemessen an der Anzahl der zu gewinnenden Delegiertenstimmen ist New Hampshire relativ unbedeutend, gleichwohl wird der Beginn des Wahlkampfes mit großem Interesse verfolgt und gibt nicht zuletzt Aufschluss darüber, wie die Chancen der parteiinternen Gegner in der Wahlkampagne sind. Hillary Clinton hat das *popular vote* gewonnen, aber sie und Obama erhalten die gleiche Anzahl von Delegiertenstimmen für die "National Convention", weil der prozentuale Anteil der auf sie entfallenden Wählerstimmen nahezu identisch war. Dennoch war der *New Hampshire Primary* besonders, weil zum ersten Mal eine Frau gewonnen hat.

Das Video der Rede kann auf *YouTube* angeschaut werden, auf Barack Obamas Website wird darauf verwiesen; die Länge des Videos beträgt 13 Minuten.

### Aufgaben

1 *What is the occasion and the purpose of this speech? Use the Internet to help you.*

2 *Describe the structure of the speech.*

3 *What stylistic and rhetorical devices does Obama use? Give examples.*

4 *How effective do you think this speech was in the 2008 presidential campaign?*

### Lösungen

1 Obama held this speech in New Hampshire after it had become clear that New Hampshire had gone to Hillary Clinton. He used this speech to present his narrow defeat as a victory – if not for himself, then for the Democrats and the people of the USA.

**2** Structure

| | |
|---|---|
| Lines 1-15 | Introduction |
| Lines 16-36 disease | Rising action, he introduces the "new America" he wants to build when he becomes president, giving examples what he'll improve. |
| Lines 37-50 | Building tension by elaborating on his vision of a "new America", giving examples from American history of how the American people are able to change things for the better. |
| Line 51 | Climax through the repetition of his slogan "Yes, we can," which almost seems like an oath. |
| Line 52-54 | Conclusion, supporting his words by more examples from the American past who stated that people who had a vision and courage built the USA. |

**3** Remarkable is his use of personal pronouns: He includes his listeners (and all of America) by using 'we' entirely when speaking of his results and addressing thus-united voters directly in the second person singular, as his comrades.

The second paragraph ends with the words "...there is something happening..." which will be the opening words in the following three paragraphs (repetition). These words are repeated three times and end the first part of the speech in line 18. Using alliteration (voices and... votes, Des Moines and Davenport) and imagery (...wait in lines that stretch block after block) he connects with the audience by referring directly to their experiences just prior to their voting. In the 6th paragraph he uses another repetition by illustrating the coming of age of 'a new majority'. The words "new majority" are repeated three times and end the second part of his speech in line 33. Using alliteration (division and distraction, ... disagree without being disagreeable) and imagery (political darkness... has clouded Washington) and vocabulary that motivates taking action (mobilize our voices to challenge) he illustrates the US' better future. Again, he uses contrasts (doctors and patients, workers and businesses...middle-class tax cuts into the pockets of the working Americans ... farmers and scientists, citizens and entrepreneurs) to show that there are no differences but only unity with the purpose to improve America's future. Obama uses imagery again describing everyday-life situations of the voters: e.g. the corridors of shame become pathways to success. He uses the personal pronoun "you" to show that he cannot be a good president without the support of the voters. In doing so, he presents himself as their leader or executive of their needs; he is not power-hungry but wants to help. Only twice, when he states that with him as president the Americans can change something, does he use "I".

Coming to the climax of his speech he clarifies to the audience that this belief is at the very heart of America, and refers to the origins of the United States and their history. He gives several examples, which are introduced and then interrupted by the words "Yes, we can". This phrase is repeated twelve times until the end of the speech, sounding like a chorus of self-affirmation directed at the audience who may be different and come from all over the country but are united in belief and pursuit of happiness and change and should not doubt that change is possible. He ends the speech referring to American tradition and values with words from the song "America, the Beautiful" from Katharine Lee Bates, a song which almost became the National Anthem of the USA in 1926 and which every American knows by heart.

**4** Individual answers. Students should recognise that Obama is hailed as an incredibly gifted orator, and was able to electrify more and more voters in the course of the campaign. All in all, Obama proves himself to be a genius in rhetoric, who is successful in uniting people in his beliefs for a better America. He manages to inspire hope and new motivation. At the end of the speech the audience has probably forgotten his defeat in New Hampshire that day. They only remember one thing: Yes, he can and will change something if I vote for him.

# Module II Wag the Dog

## **Szenenprotokoll** (Gesamtlänge 92 Min., 19 Kapitel)

| | | |
|---|---|---|
| 1 | Expression „wag the dog": Why does the dog wag its tail? Because it's smarter than the tail. If the tail wagged the dog, it would mean that the tail would be smarter than the dog." | 00:00 – 00:43 |
| 2 | Commercial „Never change horses", two jockeys talking, one gives advice to the other never to change horses in mid-stream. It turns out that this is the slogan of a campaign ad to vote for the current US president on election day. The slogan "Never change horses in mid-stream" will reappear in various different spots throughout the whole movie as a recurring motif. | 00:44 – 01:11 |
| 3 | In the White House, „Mr. Fix It"/ Brean arrives. He is led into an office by Winifred Ames, a woman working for the president, where various people wait for him. The atmosphere is secretive and Brean doesn't yet know what the meeting is about.<br>It turns out that the president sexually assaulted a female student and that an article about the incident will be in the Washington Post the next day. The president is currently in China and Brean gives orders to keep him there until the story is dealt with. Brean plans to spread the rumour that the president is in China to talk about the B-3-Bomber, an airplane that doesn't even exist. In doing so, Brean wants to distract the press for about two weeks until election day.<br>On their flight to Hollywood to meet a producer, Brean tells Ames that he worked for the Reagan administration and covered the death of 200 marines in the Gulf War with the invasion of Granada and that he's now also planning a fake war. | 01:12 – 08:36 |
| 4 | They land in Chicago. Brean has decided that they'll declare war on Albania, a country nobody knows anything about. While they wait for their connecting flight to L.A., Brean watches TV and the sexual misconduct of the president is the first thing mentioned on the news. The rumour of the B-3 bomber is started.<br>Senator Neal is the president's opponent in the election and wants the president to come home to "face the music" and let the people decide on election day. The president is 17% ahead in the polls. | 08:37 – 11:06 |
| 5 | Brean and Ames arrive at the producer's house in Hollywood. They tell Stanley the producer about the problem and that they need a distraction. At first the producer doubts that he could be of any help, but then is caught by the thrill of the whole plan. Brean compares politics to show business and explains him how to help the president: by producing a war. In return for his help he offers Stanley an ambassadorship. | 11:07 – 17:13 |
| 6 | Stanley is working out the war with Albania by finding made-up reasons for the war: they own "the bomb", they send terrorists with a nuclear bomb in a suitcase to Canada to threaten the US. He books musicians and actors for his "movie" to save the president's reputation. | 17:14 – 21:16 |
| 7 | "Think tank" about the campaign to save the president's reputation: product placement by the "gag-king" such as supporting bracelets or hat, a supportive song for soldiers in Albania, section 303, is produced. | 21:17 – 27:50 |
| 8 | The president declares a state of war between USA and the Republic of Albania. Stanley shoots a short movie/ trailer right from a faked Albanian battlefield to get the attention of the American citizens, young girl flees from soldiers with kitten in her arms after she has been raped.<br>The president arrives from China, at airport he is met by little Albanian girl with grandmother, grandmother receives president's coat. All this was planned by Stanley. | 27:51 – 35:01 |

| | | |
|---|---|---|
| 9-10 | Brean and Ames drive off to the airport, Winifred finds out that the prank worked, no newspaper is writing about the scandal anymore. They are followed by the CIA unnoticed. They are stopped and interviewed by the CIA who have solid evidence that there is no war. Brean manages to convince them that there is a war by clever "misinterpretation" of facts. | 35:02 – 43:11 |
| 11 | "War song" is produced and aired. The president's opponent, Senator Neill, "ends" the war in a short video where he states that there now is peace between the US and Albania and supports his announcement with proof of the CIA. The problem is that it is still too long to election day, and that the affair about the sexual assault might revive. | 43:12 – 48:11 |
| 12 | A new song is produced due to the new situation; thanks to the gag-king the team now focuses on a story about a soldier who is trapped behind the Canadian border. They look for and find a soldier named William Schumann in the army records and even though they don't know anything about him, the song is called "Old shoe" and Schumann is made a war hero. Song is put on an old record, which is placed in Library of Congress. | 48:12 – 51:54 |
| 13 | President is told to inform the public about Schumann's fate with a speech, team works on speech. Another election spot "Never change horses" appears on TV and it becomes obvious that the team is not the campaign team working for the president, but must be a so-called special unit. President refuses to hold the speech because he finds it too corny. Stanley holds speech to secretaries of the president, president listens and gets advice from Stanley. Secretaries leave the room crying. President reads speech to nation. Again, the viewer doesn't see the president, but only a man from behind and hears his voice. | 51:55 – 57:51 |
| 14 | Speech can be heard in the background, while Stanley and Brean drive home and watch TV in the car. It turns out that their work has paid off well, the whole nation is feeling for Willie Schumann, the soldier who has been left behind. Stanley has "campaign idea" to throw pairs of old shoes into trees as a sign of support. This idea will be taken up by the American citizens at various occasions. | 57:52 – 01:29:59 |
| 15 | The new song is found to be from 1939, when the record is found in the Library of Congress (see scene 12), polls rise to 86 % for president again. The actor Jim Belushi turns out to be Albanian and reminds his fellow countrymen to set Schumann free. Pictures of various Americans wearing patriotic T-shirts are shown. More and more shoes appear in trees. A war memorial for the war against Albania is already planned; Burger King will bring out a "Schumann" meal. | 01:30:00 – 01:05:26 |
| 16 | The real William Schumann is picked up from the airport and clearly is not the kind of war hero he should have been. Song "You have courage, mum" is played on TV, yet another new song because they made a picture where Willie Schumann wore a torn sweater in captivity, the holes saying "Courage, Mum" in Morse code on the front.<br>Schumann is delivered in chains by the army, it turns out that he is a convict who raped a nun and has to take strong anti-psychotics to control himself. They head back to Washington. Brean has already figured out an arrival scenario at the airport. | 01:05:27 – 01:14:14 |
| 17 | Washington is waiting for Schumann, the plane crashes, but there are no deaths. Ames yells at Stanley, who continuously states that "this is nothing, a piece of cake, a walk in the park" and that he can handle the situation. After they have been rescued by a Hispanic farm worker, they find a gas station in the middle of nowhere. Brean is instantly on the phone giving instructions on how to handle and explain the situation back in Washington. Schumann tries to rape the wife of the gas station owner and is shot dead. | 01:14:15 – 01:20:58 |

| | | |
|---|---|---|
| 18 | Brean, Ames and Stanley consider what to do and now make up the story that Schumann died in the war, so now he is the war hero he should have been. Song about Schumann's battalion, the 303, which never existed, is to be heard; solemn funeral of Schumann is shown. President has 89% in the polls, but not due to the Albanian story, but to the "Never change horses" commercials. Stanley and Brean say goodbye, the president is re-elected, and the jockey campaign ad from the beginning is shown. Stanley is angry about this and the fact that his hard work remains unnoticed. He wants to go public with the story. Brean tries to stop him by reminding him of the deal that he gets an ambassadorship for his work. Stanley still wants to go public to earn the credit he never got for any of his works – he never won an Oscar and badly needs attention. Stanley gets very angry and doesn't listen to Brean, who warns him about the consequences of going public. Stanley leaves after a fight; Brean makes a sign to a security guard and Stanley is led to a special car. | 01:20:59 – 01:27:52 |
| 19 | The farmer who rescued the team and Schumann after the plane crash is made an American citizen, he was an illegal immigrant and that could have caused problems. It is broadcast that Stanley died of a heart attack at his home – a fact that can be doubted. The film ends with a TV newscast about a group called "Albania, unite" who bombed a village in Albania. The president sends troops "back" into Albania to finish off the problem (which never existed). | 01:27:53 – 01:34:39 |

## Zusammenfassung der Filmhandlung

Barry Levinsons *Wag The Dog* ist für eine amerikanische politische Komödie ungewöhnlich schwarz. Der Präsident der Vereinigten Staaten hofft auf eine Wiederwahl gegen Senator Neal. Zwei Wochen vor dem Wahltag erscheint aber eine Meldung den Medien: der Präsident soll eine Minderjährige sexuell missbraucht haben. Einen Tag vor der Veröffentlichung sieht die Beraterin des Präsidenten, Winifred Ames (Anne Heche), nur einen Ausweg: Sie bestellt „Mr. Alleskleber" Conrad Brean (Robert de Niro) ins Weiße Haus. Dieser ist bekannt für die Verbreitung von Gerüchten und Manipulation von Medien im politischen Wahlkampf. Er sieht nur eine Möglichkeit: Die Sex-Skandal-Meldung muss durch eine noch schockierendere Nachricht „übertüncht" werden. Brean erfindet also einen Krieg mit Albanien. Wenn ein Krieg inszeniert wird, den es gar nicht gibt, müssen Mittel und Wege gefunden werden die Wähler vom Gegenteil zu überzeugen. Brean engagiert den Hollywood-Produzenten Stanley Motss (Dustin Hoffman). Dieser lässt sich von Brean überzeugen, einen spektakulären Krieg zu inszenieren: Motss erfindet eine junge von Terroristen vergewaltigte Albanerin, die nur noch sich und ihr Kätzchen aus ihrem Heimatdorf retten kann (Kirsten Dunst), lässt ein patriotisches Lied von dem bekannten Komponisten Willie Nelson schreiben und kann sogar einen von den Albanern gefangen genommenen Soldaten (Woody Harrelson) vorweisen. Am Ende muss Motss jedoch einsehen, dass Hollywood Fiktion bleibt und sich der Realität unterordnen muss.

# 1. Pre-viewing activities

## Worksheet 12: Interpretation of Film Poster and Title

### Didaktische Anmerkungen

"Why does a dog wag its tail? Because the dog is smarter than the tail. If the tail was smarter, it would wag the dog." So lautet das Sprichwort, welches den SuS in Gänze als Folie oder an der Tafel zur Verfügung gestellt werden sollte. Das Poster bzw. die DVD-Hülle kann den SuS gleichzeitig oder auch danach präsentiert werden. Nach der Spekulations- bzw. Interpretationsphase sollten Vorerwartungen der SuS an den Film auf Moderationskarten notiert werden, die zunächst an die Tafel geheftet werden. Diese Karten sollten bis zum Abschluss der Arbeit mit dem Film aufgehoben werden, damit die Vorerwartungen der SuS überprüft und abgeglichen werden können.

### Aufgaben

**1** *Jot down your first thoughts about the title and the poster of the movie.*

**2** *Write in ONE short sentence on your flashcard what you think the movie might be about and put your flashcard on the board.*

### Lösungen

individuelle Antworten.

## Worksheet 13: The Trailer

### Didaktische Anmerkungen

Die SuS schauen sich den Trailer zum Film an. Da der Trailer nur 30 sek. lang ist, sollte er mindestens zweimal angeschaut werden, um ein sicheres Verständnis des Inhaltes zu gewährleisten.

Der Trailer ist üblicherweise auf der DVD vorhanden. Sollte dies nicht der Fall sein, ist er auch im Internet zu finden unter *http://www.imdb.com/video/screenplay/vi920715545/*

### Aufgaben

**1** *Watch the trailer. Answer the following questions:*
**a)** *What is the plot of the movie about?* **b)** *Where does it take place?* **c)** *Who play the main characters?*

**2** *Write a short summary of the movie with just the information from the trailer as a basis.*

### Lösungen

**1a)** There is a crisis in the White House and the re-election of the current US-president has to be secured by all means. A war is faked to distract the public.
**b)** In the USA/ Washington. **c)** Dustin Hoffman, Robert DeNiro

**2** Die SuS können ihrer Phantasie fast freien Lauf lassen, da nur wenige Detailinformationen im Trailer mitgeteilt werden. Lediglich die Tatsache, dass es einen Skandal im Weißen Haus gegeben hat, der die Ablenkung durch einen fiktiven Krieg erfordert, ist vorgegeben. Welcher Art der Skandal ist, bleibt ungewiss.

## 2. While-viewing activities

### Worksheet 14: A Political Scandal

**Didaktische Anmerkungen**
Die SuS beschäftigen sich mit vergangenen politischen Skandalen in der amerikanischen Politik, die den Präsidenten – oder einen Präsidentschaftskandidaten – betrafen. In Gruppen von vier SuS werden vier verschiedene Skandale für eine Präsentation vorbereitet. Den SuS sollte die Methodik des Referates / der Präsentation bekannt sein. Die Präsentationen sollten eine Dauer von 15 Min. nicht überschreiten und sie sollten über zwei Doppelstunden verteilt werden, um die Aufmerksamkeit der Zuhörer zu gewährleisten.

Den Gruppen wird jeweils eine Internetadresse, die für die Bearbeitung des jeweiligen Themas nötig ist, die aber nur als Hilfe zum Einstieg in das Thema dienen soll. Weitere Quellen sind für eine ausreichende Präsentation des Themas notwendig.

1. The Watergate affair: *http://www.washingtonpost.com/wp-srv/politics/special/watergate/#chapters*
2. The Lewinsky scandal: *http://edition.cnn.com/ALLPOLITICS/1998/resources/lewinsky/timeline/*
3. Presidential Election 2000: *http://election2000.stanford.edu/*

**Aufgaben**
*In* Wag the Dog *the political problem is the president's sexual assault of a student in the White House. There have been scandals about US presidents in the past. Get together in groups of four and research on ONE of the following political scandals.*

**Lösungen**
Individuelle Schülerbeiträge. Wichtig ist die Herausarbeitung der historischen Bedeutung der Skandale. Richard Nixon musste nach Watergate zurücktreten, Bill Clinton musste sein Amt zwar nicht aufgeben, die Lewinsky-Affäre wird seinem Namen aber für immer anhaften, und die Präsidenten Bush und Hayes werden immer mit dem Makel des Wahlbetrügers behaftet sein.

Punktabzug sollte bei Überschreitung der Zeitvorgabe von 15 min. und bei bloßem Ablesen des Handouts gegeben werden.

### Worksheet 15: Fishbowl-Discussion

Topic: How damaging are political scandals for a nation's leader?

**Didaktische Anmerkungen**
Die SuS sollten vor Beginn der Diskussion in einem Wort an die Tafel schreiben, welchen Effekt ihrer Meinung nach ein politischer Skandal auf den politischen

Anführer einer Nation haben könnte. Die Sammlung an der Tafel dient den SuS als Diskussionsgrundlage.

Im Anschluss an diese Sammelphase wird der Kurs geteilt und die Fishbowl-Diskussion mit "Hot Seat" geführt.

**Aufgaben**
*How damaging are political scandals for a nation's leader?*

**Lösungen**
Individuelle Ergebnisse. Die Tatsache, dass politische Skandale ebenso schädliche wie kaum bemerkbare Auswirkungen auf die Politik eines Landes haben können, sollte das Ergebnis sein. Zahllose kleinere Skandale verpuffen nach einer kurzen Phase der Aufregung und das politische Geschehen geht ohne Veränderung weiter wie zuvor.

Eine schriftliche Hausaufgabe zur Frage „What will happen to the president in *Wag the Dog*" würde sich im Anschluss an die Diskussion anbieten. Die SuS wissen, dass der Wahltag kurz bevor steht und es ist anzunehmen, dass die Mehrheit davon ausgehen wird, dass er Präsident sein Amt verliert. Die Ideen der SuS, die einen Ausweg für den Präsidenten sehen, könnten als interessante Diskussionsgrundlage im Plenum dienen.

## Worksheet 16: Characters and Characterization

**Didaktische Anmerkungen**
Die SuS erhalten dieses Arbeitsblatt als Vorlage für die sich anschließende Charakterisierung von Brean, Motts und Ames. Es bietet sich an, die Charakterisierung der Hauptfiguren fortlaufend anfertigen zu lassen, da einige Charaktermerkmale erst im Verlauf des Films deutlich werden. So könnte bei jedem weiteren Anschauen des Films der Arbeitsauftrag gegeben werden Notizen zum Charakter bzw. Verhalten der Hauptfiguren anzufertigen.

**Aufgaben**
*Describe the characters of the president's staff in as much detail as possible.*

**Lösungen**

| **Conrad "Connie" Brean** | |
|---|---|
| outward appearance | • about 50 years of age<br>• always wears a hat<br>• not very neatly dressed, doesn't appear as powerful and influential as he really is |
| behaviour | • mysterious political consultant / high-end Washington spin doctor, specialized in near-impossible image rescues ➔ Mr. Fix-it (ch. 2, Ames: "That's him. That's Mr. Fix-it.")<br>• president himself called for him to fix things (ch. 3), he has already worked for the Reagan administration (ch. 3)<br>• rock-hard and self-confident<br>• never explains his exact job title or position in the president's staff (Although several other characters ask him, "What exactly is it that you do for the President".) |

| | |
|---|---|
| | • knows how to feed the press with the right information to distract them from what is really happening – president is sentenced to longer stay in China; Brean literally tells the staff what to tell the press and how to say it. (ch. 3)<br>• always knows whom to call and what to do next, here: to see a Hollywood producer to save the election (ch. 3)<br>• influential and powerful in (inter)national politics, he is able to offer Motts an ambassadorship and he seems to have unlimited access to money ("We need 20,000 $ and a car.", ch. 3)<br>• he seems to be the real leader of the American nation, a master of manipulation who is able to make the CIA question their own evidence (ch. 9)<br>• great in manipulation (ch. 4 the way he makes up Albania's hostile position to the USA), manipulates press conferences to focus attention on the non-existant B-3 bomber and away from the real problem<br>• Fast thinker, quickly switches between solutions, when plan A fails he immediately comes up with plan B – when Schumann turns out to be psychotic he immediately gets on the phone and tells the president's PR department what to tell the public (ch. 3, 4:00)<br>• "works" on Motss, follows him for a day to convince him<br>• you NEVER now whether he is telling the truth or not<br>• atmosphere of danger surrounds him, he tells Tracey with a smile that she'll be killed if she ever tells anyone about her job in the film (ch. 8)<br>• "peak" of manipulative skills when he puts a new record into the Library of Congress and makes it look antique (ch. 12, 51:50)<br>• people listen to him without any hesitance, when he tells a young press woman from the president's staff to sleep with someone from CBS she gets herself information about the "old shoe" (ch. 14, 58:30)<br>• threatens to kill Motss or have him killed if he ever tells anything about the "old shoe" campaign (ch. 17, 1:16) |
| words and thoughts | • "It doesn't matter if it's true, it's a story, if it breaks, we have to run backwards." (ch. 3)<br>• "I'm working on it."<br>• "A good plan today is better than a perfect plan tomorrow."<br>• „What difference does it make if it's true? If it's a story and it breaks, they're gonna run with it."<br>• „(War) is show business. That's why we're here. ... Gulf War? Smart bomb, falling down a chimney. Twenty-five-hundred missions a day, 100 days, one video of one bomb Mr. Motss. The American people bought that war."<br>• "Producing is like being a plumber." (ch. 14)<br>• "...blablabla" (telling people what to tell the press) |
| others' reactions | • president obeys his orders (stays in China as instructed)<br>• more powerful and influential than Winifred Ames, the president's PR woman, cuts her off various times, which she accepts |
| feelings and attitudes | • cold blooded, sacrifices Schumann and Motss without any regrets, it seems to be part of the job for him<br>• there is no truth for him, truth is what the people believe and what he wants them to believe.<br>• may worry that Motss is better than him, after the "old shoe" has more success than his Albanian campaign |
| **Stanley Motss** | |
| outward appearance | • successful Hollywood producer,<br>• in his fifties, looks after his health (ch. 4 "Veggie Shake", plays tennis), wants to look younger (ch. 4, tanning)<br>• self-confident due to his success in the film industry<br>• self-infatuated, comic portrait of extraordinary freshness and satiric force<br>• likes luxurious home, car, clothes<br>• loud appearance |

| | |
|---|---|
| behaviour | • vain, not only concerning his looks but also his reputation, he wants everybody to know what he did for the president (ch. 4, he tells Brean, and only pulls back when he realizes that it could be dangerous)<br>• doesn't care about anybody he works with (ch. 8, instantly forgets that actress' name is Tracey, not Stacey)<br>• eccentric who likes big gestures, swears a lot (ch. 4: "This guy is fucked."), wants people to listen to him, doesn't care if the president is on the phone, when he's speaking it's more important (ch. 6)<br>• doesn't believe the president's situation could be improved (ch. 5), when Brean proves his influence with a phone call (ch. 5, 14:05) he gets excited.<br>• high self-esteem, making a campaign-film is routine for him<br>• treats project like a "normal" film production with product placements, merchandise products (ch. 14, even a memorial and a clock are planned ch. 15) and so on (ch. 7 national dish (Albanian restaurant, Jim Belushi), Burger King should produce "shoe burger" (ch. 15)<br>• creative, effective, he has the ideas, Brean has the contacts to make them real<br>• together with his creative team and songwriter, he treats the campaign Brean has ordered him to work on like an advertising campaign complete with theme song, heart-tugging symbols and scenes of action that go directly from a Hollywood soundstage to CNN.<br>• quick thinker, great ideas, as good as Brean in coming up with plans B and C (ch. 11, start of "old shoe" campaign)<br>• he is the one who gets the war going : "We just found out that they have the (suitcase) bomb/ Albanian Terrorists have placed a suitcase Bomb in Canada, in an attempt to infiltrate the bomb into the USA." (ch. 6)<br>• wants credit, even the ambassadorship Brean offers him is not as interesting as finally being respected by the film industry<br>• becomes almost as powerful as Brean, it's him who convinces the president to hold the corny speech "Courage Mom" (ch. 14)<br>• marketing of "campaign" thought through thoroughly, throwing away old shoes for "old shoe" William Schuman means that people have to buy new shoes (ch. 14: "We have some new powerful friends in the association of international shoe manufacturers." 59:54)<br>• his marketing strategies are almost always successful, throwing away of shoes becomes national "duty", patriotism of American citizens with (non-existant) captured soldier is rising (ch. 15)<br>• is the only one to keep cool when they have to deal with the "problem" William Schumann (ch. 16: "When a guy comes back from combat and torture, of course he's gonna be fucked up." (1:11)<br>• refuses to accept that he can't ever tell the real story about the "old shoe" campaign (ch. 17, 1:16)<br>• when Schumann is killed he becomes a war hero and his homecoming is even more triumphant ➔ it was Motss' and Brean's idea (ch. 18) |
| words and thoughts | • "When it's cookin', it's cookin." (new project)<br>• "This is nothing." (serious problem or failure of a plan)<br>• „...this is nothing. This is nothing. ..., this is a walk in the park..."<br>• "This is politics at its finest."<br>• "This is a complete fucking fraud and it looks 100% real. That's the best work I've ever done in my life – because it's so honest." (ch. 18)<br>• "I made this lame turkey fly, I did it pure Hollywood." (ch. 18)<br>• "I want the credit." (ch. 18) |
| others' reactions | • Ames and Brean are first fascinated by his manipulative skills, but then annoyed by his jovial behaviour (ch. 6, 20:11) and fear his skills in the end when they notice that without him they wouldn't have won the election<br>• when he wants credit for his work, Brean wants to stop him going public and threatens to have him killed when Motss refuses to keep quiet |

| | |
|---|---|
| feelings and attitudes | • easily frustrated – when the war is ended even though the song just has been finished it's no problem<br>• becomes megalomaniac (ch. 11, "They can't end the war, it's my picture,…. now we need an act 2"., ch. 15 "I should hold the inaugural speech" (1:03:53)<br>• starts to feel superior to everybody (ch. 11 :"They don't know who they're playing with.")<br>• Brean has to convince him to work for the president<br>• he begins to think that campaigns are his thing (ch. 15)<br>• gets caught up in the campaign, doesn't realize that this is not a film but politics<br>• sees this as the opportunity of a lifetime, a chance to use his high-powered skills to manipulate not just a movie audience, but the entire country by playing foul<br>• Motss and Brean are quite alike, they are brilliant thinkers, very creative and fast (ch. 12, 50:55) ➔ that's why only one of them can live and Brean is then a bit smarter than Motss/ colder than Motss<br>• Motss gets even more "dangerous" for Brean when he is able to convince the president of the corny speech while Brean isn't (ch. 13) and when he's the one to tell Ames what to do about the illegal immigrant who saved them after their plane crash (ch. 17)<br>• cold-blooded, doesn't care about Schumann being killed (ch. 17), is only worried about his campaign<br>• unhappy that he has never won an Oscar (ch. 18) and very disappointed when he finds out his "film" wasn't the reason why the president was re-elected but the really bad "Never change horses in mid-stream." campaign<br>• dies of a heart attack at the end of the movie , it can be assumed that he was killed on Brean's orders (ch. 19)<br>• deeply hurt when he finds out that it was the commercials which won the president the $2^{nd}$ term (ch. 18, 1:25), he wants the credit and not an ambassadorship or money<br>• weak self-esteem becomes clear when he is outraged at the fact that the whole "film" has to stay secret (ch. 18) |
| **Winifred Ames** | |
| outward appearance | • blonde woman in her mid-thirties<br>• the president's PR consultant<br>• neatly but rather formally dressed, tidy hair and make-up |
| behaviour | • she's the one who calls Mr. Fix-It for help because the president told her to do so (ch. 2/3)<br>• always on her mobile phone, either giving instruction or talking to the president<br>• sometimes hysterical, especially when under pressure<br>• sometimes over-correct (man who picked them up after the plane crash in a harvester was an illegal alien without a green card – he has to get American citizenship so everything is correct and can't be appealed against)<br>• when she first meets Brean she feels superior to him but she quickly realizes that Brean's the one in charge<br>• likes to be in charge, but others interrupt her (ch. 3) ➔ her position is weaker than she thinks it is<br>• admires Brean for his ideas (ch. 10), she becomes his executive tool, she can't stop or control his actions when he tells the songwriter he can earn a lot of money (ch. 6)<br>• smoker<br>• "chickens out" when CIA finds out about the fraud (ch. 10, "I'm on medication.")<br>• moves clumsily (ch. 17, 1:20)<br>• easy to convince – when Brean suggests a war she first says that the US cannot afford a war but when he tells her about what he – might have – done about the Gulf War she changes her mind and cooperates (ch. 3)<br>• lies / manipulates when she has to (ch. 8, tells actress that signature is for her insurance (an obvious lie) |

| | |
|---|---|
| | • works for gratitude of party and president (ch. 15, 1:05)<br>• left helpless by Brean and Motss when there are problems she has to deal with (ch. 16 when William Schumann turns out to be a psychotic convict)<br>• loses her temper when plain crashes and all seems to be lost, swears at Motss and blames him (ch. 17) |
| words and thoughts | • "You could talk a bone out of a dog"<br>• "What have you done to me", the only time she complains to Brean when Schumann turns out to be a madman (ch. 16)<br>• "(TV) destroyed the electoral process." (ch. 17)<br>• "So close and yet so far." (ch. 18, when she "mourns" Schumann's death) |
| others' reactions | • Brean cuts her off various times, even though she's the one working for the president (ch. 13, she seems to have lost her superiority, she only does what Brean tells her) |
| feelings and attitudes | • single mother of a 3 year old daughter<br>• hyper-nervous, helpless in the face of the manipulative Brean and Motss<br>• loyal to president, when Motss continuously talks about the credit he wants for his job she tells him that the party's and the president's gratitude is more important than anything else and that should be enough |

Brean and Ames are flat characters; they don't change but stick to their principles, they are cold-blooded and without any scruples on their way to the presidency from the beginning on.

Motss on the other hand changes from cool and evil-loving Hollywood producer to an offended artist who is not getting enough credit for what he has done.

## Worksheet 17: Scene Analysis: The Opening Scene

### Didaktische Anmerkungen

Die SuS analysieren die Anfangsszene des Films. Diese lässt nur wenige Spekulationen über den weiteren Inhalt des Filmes zu. Es wird Spannung erzeugt durch die Aufnahmen der Überwachungskamera und den hektisch Treppen herunter laufenden Menschen. Der Wechsel der Bilder zwischen denen der Überwachungskamera und dem wirklichen Geschehen lassen die dargestellte Unruhe auf den Zuschauer übergehen. Die Szene ist somit geeignet, um den Einsatz filmischer Mittel zu untersuchen und die Szene dann zu analysieren.

### Aufgaben

**1** *Watch the first scene of the movie (ch. 3, 1:25-3:05) and focus on the following aspects: Action, Characters & Cinematic Devices & their Functions*

**2** *Now that you've gathered information interpret the scene, giving reasons why the director chose to open the movie with it.*

**3** *Give your personal opinion about the scene. Does it leave an impression? Does it make you want to keep watching?*

**Lösungen**

**1**

| | |
|---|---|
| Action | ➔ time and place: the White House, late at night (it's dark)<br>➔ atmosphere: suspense, tension, Mr. Fix-It is greeted with a nod only, people of unknown profession still in the rooms of the White House, it is obviously night, there's only security and cleaning staff still there<br>➔ events: unknown man "Mr. Fix-It" being checked by security guards and finally admitted to a room in the basement where other people are waiting for him, hardly any conversation on their hectic way downstairs |
| Characters | ➔ description of characters: Mr. Fix-It (Robert de Niro), beardy man with hat, 2 women waiting for him who are neatly dressed, (Anne Heche, other actress of minor importance, not known by name), people waiting in the basement office dressed rather formally<br>➔ impression on the viewer:<br>*Brean*: awkward outward appearance with hat, knitted sweater, jeans and bow tie, doesn't seem to be intimidated by the security checks though, nor by the fact that he's led into a "secret" office in the basement of the White House.<br>*Ames*: dressed rather formally, confident while leading Brean into the basement, showing him where to take a seat and introducing him, conversation reduced to a minimum; cuts from the security cameras and "real" pictures |
| Cinematic devices and their function | ➔ camera operations (field sizes, movements, positions, angles): *field sizes*: long shot (when Brean comes in), extreme close-up (hoover, feet walking down the stairs), medium shot (when Ames and her female colleague are first shown),<br>*camera movements*: tracking shot (in the basement on their way to the secret office), horizontal pan (when they're on their way downstairs), static shot (when Brean comes in, while they're walking down the stairs)<br>*camera positions*: reverse angle shot, over-the-shoulder shot (when Brean is greeted by the two women)<br>*camera angles*: eye-level shot when they're in the basement about to reach their destination low-angle shot<br>➔ symbols: the White House<br>➔ music, sounds: guitar music, bits of conversation, footsteps |

**2** The students should point out that suspense is created through the mixture of surveillance camera and "real" pictures, as well as through the walk down the stairs. The viewer can only see feet walking down stairs very quickly; there seems to be a feeling of urgency, but the viewer doesn't yet know why. The establishing shot at the beginning of the scene gives an overview; the viewer is immediately introduced to the scene of the action, the White House. The director limited the characters to three, one of them being the mysterious Mr. Fix-It (the viewer doesn't yet know what he has to fix). The low-angle shot in the dark basement corridor creates an increase in suspense; the women escorting Brean to some secret place/ office look more important and powerful through this perspective. This power is only of short duration, as the viewer quickly learns as the movie proceeds; Brean is the man in charge.

The scene is well-chosen to keep the viewer watching, he wants to find out what is going on in the White House at night and what Mr. Fix-It has to fix. It becomes clear that there's secrecy involved and viewers are curious to find out what needs to be taken care of, especially in the light of the presidential election.

**3** individual answers

## Worksheet 18: The War Begins

### Didaktische Anmerkungen

Für dieses Arbeitsblatt sollte eine Doppelstunde zur Verfügung stehen. Die SuS beschäftigen sich mit der Produktion der Kriegsberichterstattung aus Albanien von Stanley Motss. Zunächst lesen sie nur den Teil des Drehbuchs der Szene, der sich mit den Vorbereitungen der Filmaufnahmen beschäftigt. Im Anschluss an die Lesephase äußern die SuS ihren ersten Eindruck. Besondere Aufmerksamkeit soll der Atmosphäre und dem Verhältnis zwischen Ames, Brean und Motss gewidmet werden.

Die SuS sollen dann den Fernsehbericht selbst in Gruppen erarbeiten und die kurzen Szenen dem Plenum vorstellen. Besonderheiten wie bestimmte Requisiten oder Spezialeffekte werden an der Tafel notiert, damit sie später mit dem eigentlichen Spot verglichen werden können. Die SuS sollen ihr eigenes Wissen über Kriegsberichterstattung einbringen und ihren Spot ähnlich gestalten

Nach der Darstellung der von den SuS erarbeiteten Spots schließt sich eine kurze Lesephase an, in welcher der zweite Teil des Drehbuches der Szene gelesen wird und die SuS erfahren, wie der von Motss produzierte Spot ausgesehen hat. Der erste Eindruck könnte mit der Methode des Blitzlichtes gesammelt werden: Jeder S spricht nur über seinen persönlichen Eindruck. Die Wortbeiträge sind nicht länger als ein bis zwei Sätze. Während ein S sich äußert, hören die anderen ausschließlich zu, es dürfen lediglich Verständnisfragen gestellt werden. Auch werden getroffene Äußerungen nicht kommentiert, kritisiert oder bewertet oder zum Anlass einer Diskussion genommen.

Die SuS schauen sich dann den Spot und die sich anschließende Berichterstattung in den Nachrichten an. Es sollte dann die Gelegenheit bestehen die SuS zu fragen, ob sich ihr erster Eindruck nun, nachdem sie die Bilder zum Drehbuch gesehen haben, verändert hat. Zum Abschluss der Arbeit mit dem Filmausschnitt wird das Verhältnis zwischen Ames, Brean und Motss näher untersucht, hier könnten auch die von den SuS schon angefertigten Charakterisierungen der drei Hauptfiguren ergänzt werden.

### Aufgaben

**1** *Watch the scene from "Wag the Dog" (ch. 8, 28:17-31:15). Describe the atmosphere at the film set. Pay special attention to the relationship between Ames, Brean and Motss.*

**2** *The stage is set for shooting the actual newscast. Get together in groups and continue the screenplay individually actually "shooting" the report for the national evening news on US television.*

**3** *Now watch the report Stanley Motss produced. How does this report underline Motss' ingenuity as a producer?*

### Lösungen

**1** The atmosphere is hectic and uncomfortable: the big blue room without any props, many people running around hastily, talking into headsets or mobile phones and Motss' confusing instructions. There is no music at all. The atmosphere becomes threatening and awkward when Brean tells Tracy that if she ever tells anyone she helped in the fraud she will be killed. He does that with a smile on his face, which shows how dangerous and powerful he really is. Ames becomes a partner for Brean, she lies to Tracy when she wants her signature. The viewer doesn't know what Tracy has to sign but can be sure that it doesn't have anything to do with her insurance. Concerning the relationship between the three main protagonists, the students should notice that in spite of the fact that Motss is the producer of the spot, Ames and Brean are the ones in charge. They are just using Motss' connections, equipment and vanity for their purposes.

**2** individual answers

**3** Motss is a man who has his aim in focus at all times and is used to getting what he wants. At the film set, everybody listens to him, he's the one making decisions concerning stage directions and actors. His team listens to his ideas, even though they are out of place – he is talking about water, a second later about a calico kitten, the technician reacts instantly. He knows which sounds to add to the picture and which special effects to use. He knows he's good and when he isn't told so enough, he blows his own trumpet in saying that he has an instinct for casting concerning Tracy's Albanian look. When there's someone else making decisions he has to listen to – like the president wanting a white kitten – he is angry and upset. His vanity and egocentricity contribute to the "genius" image he has cultivated.

## Worksheet 19: After the War

### Didaktische Anmerkungen

Obwohl Brean die CIA davon überzeugt zu haben scheint, dass sich die USA im Krieg gegen Albanien befinden, verkündet der Herausforderer Senator Neal, dass der Krieg mit Albanien beendet worden ist und fordert eine Stellungnahme des Präsidenten. Diese Neuigkeiten treffen das Team mitten in der Chorprobe des Propagandasongs für die Soldaten im Kampfeinsatz und alles scheint verloren.

Die SuS schauen sich den Film bis zu der Verkündung des Kriegsendes von Senator Neal und den sich anschließenden niedergeschlagenen Äußerungen von Brean und Ames. Im Anschluss sollen sie darüber spekulieren, wie der Film weitergehen könnte. Die Ergebnisse dieser kurz zu haltenden Phase werden auf Moderationskarten gesammelt, an die Tafel geheftet und von einem bis zwei SuS – je nach Kursgröße – geclustert. Eine kurze Diskussion der Ideen sollte sich anschließen. Auch diese Moderationskarten sollten von der Lehrkraft aufgehoben werden, um sie später mit dem tatsächlichen Fortgang des Filmes vergleichen zu können.

Der zweite Arbeitsauftrag spricht die Kreativität und Phantasie der SuS an. Sie sollen sich in die Person von Motss hineinversetzen und eine Lösung des Problems erarbeiten. Die SuS erarbeiten in Gruppen eine neue Kampagne – die zeitliche Vorgabe sollte 15 Minuten nicht überschreiten – und stellt diese in kurzen Präsentationen von maximal 5 Minuten Dauer dem Plenum vor. Auch diese Ergebnisse sollten gesichert werden, um sie mit der Filmhandlung vergleichen zu können.

## Worksheet 20: Analysis of Campaign Ads

### Didaktische Anmerkungen

Die SuS analysieren die Wahlkampfvideos des Präsidenten mit dem Slogan "Never change horses in mid-stream" hinsichtlich der eingesetzten filmischen Mittel und dem Text. Abschließend beurteilen sie die Videos auf ihren Effekt auf die Wähler. Die Videos sollten zunächst in Gruppenarbeit einzeln analysiert werden und die Ergebnisse an der Tafel gesichert werden. Im Anschluss sollte sich eine Diskussion darüber anschließen, warum die Wahlkampfvideos als Grund für die Wiederwahl des Präsidenten angesehen werden, wie von den Experten in der Talkshow (Kap. 18) behauptet. Die vier Werbespots decken verschiedene Themen des Wahlkampfes ab: Familienpolitik, Wirtschaft, Sicherheit und die US-amerikanische Vormachtstellung in der Weltpolitik. Des Weiteren werden Rentner und Afroamerikaner in den Spots dargestellt, um eine möglichst große Bandbreite der US-amerikanischen Bevölkerung zu erreichen. Die SuS werden erkennen, dass die Spots altmodisch wirken und ihre Produktion nahezu laienhaft. Warum diese Spots dem Präsidenten dennoch zur Wiederwahl verholfen haben soll von den SuS herausgearbeitet werden. Im Ergebnis steht, dass die Art der Produktion unwichtig zu sein scheint, solange den Wählern ein Gefühl der Sicherheit gegeben wird. Dieses Gefühl der Sicherheit vermitteln die Spots, sicherlich auch in Verbindung mit dem „gewonnen Krieg gegen Albanien." Dass der Präsident mit Hilfe der Spots wiedergewählt worden wäre, wenn Brean und Motss keine rettende Kampagne entworfen hätten, ist relativ unwahrscheinlich.

Bei einer Zeitreserve bietet es sich an dieser Stelle an, die Wahlkampfvideos aus dem Film mit denen echter Präsidentschaftskandidaten (z. B. Obama und McCain) zu vergleichen. Wenngleich diese professioneller hergestellt worden sind werden sich Ähnlichkeiten z. B. in den Themen finden lassen.

### Aufgaben

There are four different campaign ads for the re-election of the president. Get together in groups and analyse ONE of the ads in the following manner:

**1** *Analyse the use of cinematic devices in the following manner:*
- *a) Which field sizes were used?*
- *b) Which camera movements were used?*
- *c) Which camera positions were used?*
- *d) Which camera angles were used?*
- *e) How are shots linked or edited*
- *f) How is music used?*

**2** *Now that you've got the film techniques, analyse in what way they cause an effect on the viewer to re-elect the president.*

**3** *Give your personal opinion about the campaign ad you have worked with.*

### Lösungen

**1a)** full shot: extreme close-up when words "Don't change horses in mid stream." are spoken, close-up, medium shot

**b)** tracking shot, zoom in when slogan is said, pan from left to right when two men are talking to each other
**c)** establishing shot, from behind at the end of ad
**d)** eye-level shot
**e)** only pans are used, almost looks like a "home (made) video"
**f)** Soft music can be heard throughout the complete ad, becoming louder and almost triumphant ad the end of the ad with the slogan "Keep America working. Don't change horses in mid-stream. On election day re-elect the president."

**2** They create a feeling of safety and comfort, the viewer feels looked after and taken care of by the current president who doesn't take risks and wants to stabilize the country

**3** individual answers, but the video doesn't look like a professional campaign ad. There aren't any special effects, on the contrary, the close up blurs scene and makes the video look rather old-fashioned or even unprofessional:

1st ad (ch. 2, beginning of the movie): 2 jockeys talking about a derby, main slogan „Always stick with the winner."
2nd ad (ch. 7, 25:40): elderly couple having coffee in their home, main slogan "Don't change things that don't have to be changed.
3rd ad (ch. 13, 53:37): African American woman talking to her baby, main slogan: "For the future of our families, don't change horses."
4th ad: (ch. 15, 1:04:22): 2 neighbours talking about why the vote for the president: "No surprises these days." main slogan: "For an economy you can rely on."

## Worksheet 21: The Burial of a War Hero

### Didaktische Anmerkungen

Die SuS sollen sich mit dem Marschlied beschäftigen, das während der Beerdigung von William Schumann zu hören ist. Es bietet sich an, die DVD über eine Stereoanlage laufen zu lassen und den SuS die Bilder zunächst vorzuenthalten, damit sie sich nur auf den Text konzentrieren. Zu einem späteren Zeitpunkt werden selbstverständlich auch die dazugehörigen Bilder analysiert.

Die SuS hören erst einmal nur das Lied, ohne den Text vor Augen zu haben. Sie sollen dann eine kurze mündliche Zusammenfassung des Liedes abgeben, aus der sich eine kurze Diskussion darüber ergeben sollte, um welche Art von Lied es sich handelt und bei welcher Gelegenheit solche Lieder zu hören sind. Erst dann wird ihnen der Liedtext präsentiert und sie bekommen ein Arbeitsblatt mit Aufgaben zur Textanalyse. Den SuS sollte das Lied noch einmal vorgespielt werden, da die Melodie für die Analyse des Liedtextes wichtig ist. Die SuS sollten dazu Stellung nehmen können, ob sich ihr Eindruck von dem Lied nach dem Hören verändert hat. Der Begriff *marching song* wird höchstwahrscheinlich fallen und sollte vom Lehrer sofort aufgegriffen und gegebenenfalls erklärt werden, da er bei der weiteren Arbeit benötigt wird. Zum Abschluss wird das Begräbnis von Schumann nochmals angesehen und das Lied auf seine Funktion als Hintergrundmusik der Szene untersucht. Bei der Beantwortung der Frage wird eine abschließende Interpretation und Bewertung des Liedes vorgenommen.

In der Hausaufgabe sollen die SuS sich die *Ballad of the Green Berets* auf *Youtube* anhören und anschauen. Sie wird von einem Mitglied der Green Berets gesungen und die SuS werden schnell erkennen, dass die Melodien der beiden Lieder identisch sind. Beide Lieder sollen miteinander verglichen werden, da *God Bless the Men of the 303* eine Persiflage auf die *Ballad of the Green Berets* ist.

**Aufgaben**

**1** *Listen closely to the song and try to understand as much of the text as possible. What is your first impression? Do you like the song?*

**2** *What is the song about? Is it a special of song?*

**3** *Now read the lyrics of the song and analyse it in more detail.*

**4** *Now that you know the lyrics, has your impression of the song changed?*

**5** *Watch the burial of William Schumann (ch. 18, 01:21:20 – 01:22:30) at which the song of the "303" can be heard. Now that you've already analysed the song, pay close attention to the pictures, namely*
**a)** *the course of the funeral service*
**b)** *the soldiers' clothes*

**6** *Comment on the song as background music for William Schumann's funeral.*

**7** *Compare the Ballad of the Green Berets and God Bless the Men of the 303 focusing on the following aspects:*
**a)** *Name the differences.*
**b)** *Comment on the songs' genre as marching songs. Which one serves its purpose better and why?*

**Lösungen**

**1** individual answers.

**2** The battalion of the 303 of which William Schumann was a member and who fought against Albania.

**3** The fictitious battalion of the 303 was invented by Stanley Motss and his team. They sing about their duties as soldiers ("with a cross to bear") and their mission ("that this great land will remain free"). The term "a cross to bear" is a symbol for a test of faith or strength, in many cases imposed by destiny. The men of the 303 are the best men in the military and with God's blessing they will protect their country. These above-average soldiers accomplish their missions in the air, on land and on the sea. In terms of the Lord's Prayer they ask for good looks in combat, wearing leopard skin hats. This seems to be of greater importance than a prayer for protection in combat.

**4** Individual answers, the students should have found out though, that this marching song is rather peculiar, because of the fact that the battalion of the 303 has never fought in any war.

**5a)** The song begins when William Schumann's coffin is lifted up and carried towards a podium in a hangar at the airport by his "comrades"/ members of the 303 unit in the special 303 uniform. It is not only played as background music underlining the scene, but there also is a marching band playing the song at the

funeral. It stops when the camera moves off from the funeral back to Motss and Brean surveying the scenery from an office in the hangar.
**b)** Berets with leopard skin and matching neckties, brown jackets and pants with braces, many patches and badges on hat and jacket, many small pockets on jacket and pants which is quite unusual for a uniform. Especially the berets and the neckties look more like a costume than a uniform.

**6** The song is a marching song that is normally sung in combat to cheer up and motivate the soldiers. Marching songs are dedicated to certain departments of the army, there is no single marching song but one for every "unit" such as Marines, Navy and Air force. William Schumann "belonged" to the 303 and his death affects every single member of this unit, his comrades are mourning his loss. Of course, there is no loss of a comrade and we don't know where the soldiers who are present at the funeral come from or who they are. There are other members of the army present at the funeral. It must be doubted that they know that the 303 is a fictitious battalion, they too are mourning the death of a soldier and comrade in combat. The song underlines the solemn atmosphere at the funeral. Men with hard faces carry the coffin, the drums in the music matching the rhythm of their footsteps. The dog Conrad Brean ordered to be present at the funeral appears when the lyric "side by side we know no fear" can be heard and the dog was ordered by Brean as a symbol for true friendship and comradeship. While the lyrics in the first two stanzas are appropriate for a marching song the third stanza sounds very strange. The first line of the third stanza is peculiar, and is directly taken from the Lord's Prayer. It seems as if the composer of the song ran out of ideas for lyrics. But in combination with the next line, in which they ask for unusual hats (the stylist, a member of Motss' team, probably chose leopard skin because it is a symbol for an aggressive warrior) the ironic character of the song becomes clear: there are no fighting men; there is nothing special about the 303 but their uniforms and thus there is no "real" marching song.

**7a)**

**God Bless The Men of the 303**
© Written by Huey Lewis, performed by Scott Matthews, Johnny Colla and Huey Lewis., Wag The Dog 1997

| God Bless The Men of the 303 | Comments |
|---|---|
| We're gathered here,<br>With a cross to bear<br>The bravest men<br>Anywhere,<br>That this great land<br>Will remain free,<br>God bless the men<br>Of the 303 | which "cross" exactly is not explained; a hollow claim which sounds like a complaint<br>bravery not defined in more detail, what they do, how they fight |

| | |
|---|---|
| Side by side<br>We know no fear,<br>Our minds are sharp,<br>Our eyes are clear.<br>In the air, on land<br>Or on the sea,<br>We're the fighting men<br>Of the 303. | too little detail<br>there are no military regiments which cover air, land and sea |
| 303<br>Give us this day<br>Our daily bread,<br>And leopard skin<br>For our head,<br>That we may fight ... | text from the Lord's Prayer, (has the lyricist run out of ideas?)<br>then becomes ridiculous, begging for leopard skin, a symbol for aggressive warriors in primitive cultures, where leopard skin was worn by chiefs or healers<br><br>they have never fought and never will |

**Ballad of the Green Berets,** © *SSgt Barry Sadler by kind permission of Americana Books*

The United States Army Special Forces, known as the Green Berets, is a Special Operations Force of the United States Army, which has five primary missions: unconventional warfare, foreign internal defense, special reconnaissance, direct action, and counter-terrorism. Their official motto is *de oppresso liber*, (to liberate the oppressed.)

| **Ballad of the Green Berets** | **Comments** |
|---|---|
| Fighting soldiers from the sky<br>Fearless men who jump and die<br>Men who mean just what they say<br>The brave men of the Green Beret | definition of what a Green Beret does: they are parachutists in combat, fearless of death |
| Silver wings upon their chest<br>These are men, America's best<br>One hundred men we'll test today<br>But only three win the Green Beret | closer definition of a Green Beret, he has to pass difficult tests to become a GB, thus he belongs to an elite unit of the armed forces |
| Trained to live, off nature's land<br>Trained in combat, hand to hand<br>Men who fight by night and day<br>Courage deep, from the Green Beret | more definition of the character of a GB and a "job description" |
| Silver wings upon their chest<br>These are men, America's best<br>One hundred men we'll test today<br>But only three win the Green Beret | GB reward for outstanding accomplishments, only a small number of applicants is good enough to become a GB, thus they can really call themselves America's best |
| Back at home a young wife waits<br>Her Green Beret has met his fate<br>He has died for those oppressed<br>Leaving her this last request | a GB must be willing to die to save and free others, this must be his highest aim and duty |

| | |
|---|---|
| Put silver wings on my son's chest<br>Make him one of America's best<br>He'll be a man they'll test one day<br>Have him win the Green Beret | recurring symbol for an elite, a "medal" which has to be earned by bravery<br>green beret as a reward that has to be honoured, the son shall follow in the father's footsteps and take revenge for his death |

**b)** The Ballad of the Green Berets is a marching song for a real special unit of the US armed services. Only very skilled soldiers become members of the GB, the song explains the GB's purposes and what has to be done to become a GB. The song displays pride in being the true and incontestable elite. Being a member of this elite even lets death in combat look less sad. The soldier has died freeing the oppressed, heroically fulfilling his mission. This is the true meaning of being a GB.

God bless the men of the 303 is a parody on marching songs. The first two stanzas are sequences of platitudes. Every soldier is brave and in the military it is not "a cross to bear" for a soldier to fight for his country, but his duty and an even an honour. This line in particular sounds like a complaint, which is rather odd for a marching song which is supposed to motivate the soldiers in combat. Still they claim to be the bravest men anywhere, who will take care of America's freedom. The second stanza consists of even more cants; sharp minds and clear eyes are neither sufficient for a soldier nor a special skill or feature. Additionally, the unit fight "everywhere", which is not the practice of the armed forces – there are special units for the land, sky and sea, namely Marines, Navy and Air force. In the second stanza the listener still doesn't know what the function of the 303 is. The third stanza ridicules marching songs, mocking the Ballad of the Green Berets begging for special hats – a reference to the Green Berets with their silver wings badge.

The songwriter Huey Lewis purposely chose the melody of the Ballad of the Green Berets for his song mocking marching songs as the director of the movie mocks political campaigns in presidential elections.

## 3. Post-viewing activities

### Worksheet 22: Politicians: Powerful Leaders or Puppets of the Media?

#### Didaktische Anmerkungen

Die SuS charakterisieren den Präsidenten und Senator Neal und beurteilen die Eignung der beiden Kandidaten für die Präsidentschaft. Senator Neal ist nicht nur häufiger im Film zu sehen als der Präsident, der Zuschauer erlebt ihn auch unmittelbar: er sagt, was er meint und tritt selbst vor die Kameras, anstatt sein Wahlkampfteam vorzuschicken. Der Präsident ist in einer Szene von Ferne zu sehen und in einer anderen nur von hinten, während der Rede in Kapitel 13 ist wiederum nur der Hinterkopf schemenhaft zu sehen und seine Stimme zu hören. Die SuS erkennen, dass der Präsident zwar Oberhaupt der mächtigsten Nation der Welt ist, aber eigentlich nichts „zu melden" hat bzw. nur dass, was sein PR-Team zulässt, wie z. B. die Auswahl der Kätzchens für den Spot über den Albanien Krieg. Während der Präsident wie eine Marionette wirkt, die für einen positiven Eindruck in den Medien durch das PR-Team in die eine oder andere Richtung bewegt wird, symbolisiert Senator Neal den ehrlichen und für das Wohl seines Landes engagierten Politiker.

Die Rede des Präsidenten aus Kapitel 13 wird von den SuS detailliert analysiert. Die SuS sollen Stilmittel heraussuchen und dann begründen dann, warum die Rede so erfolgreich war – davon ist auszugehen, nachdem die „Testzuhörerinnen" von der Rede tief berührt waren. Die gründliche Analyse dient schon der Vorbereitung der Klausur, in welcher das Gespräch zwischen Conrad Brean und dem CIA-Agenten Young aus Kapitel 10 analysiert werden soll.

Als Hausaufgabe sollen die SuS sich mit der Aussage der Journalistin in der Talkshow in Kapitel 18, 01:24:33: *„The president is a product."* beschäftigen. Hier können aktuelle Bezüge einbezogen und so auf Modul 1 zurückgegriffen werden: wie war der Wahlkampf von Obama und McCain gestaltet, welche Außenwirkung hat Obama in seiner Stellung als Präsident der USA dank erfolgreicher PR-Strategien.

**Aufgaben**

Now that you've watched the complete movie, focus on the politicians Senator Neal and the president.

**1** *Characterize Senator Neal and the president in key words only with aspects you remember from the movie.*

**2** *Which one of them seems to be more able to be the leader of a nation as powerful and influential as the USA?*

**3** *Analyse the president's "corny" speech on TV about William Schumann's captivity in chapter 13, 54:55 – 58:35.*

**a)** *Analyse the structure of the speech and find stylistic devices that support the appealing character of the speech.*

**b)** *Elaborate why the speech was so touching and thus helpful for the president's re-election.*

**4** *In chapter 18 the talk show hostess says that "The president is a product." Comment on this statement with reference to the current president of the USA, Barack Obama.*

**Lösungen**

**1**

| Senator Neal | The President |
|---|---|
| – appears in the movie more often than the president:<br>1. ch. 3, 6:12: election commercial showing the White House, background music / song "It's like heaven for little girls", main slogan "The presidency is about honesty, principles and it's about integrity. Vote Neal for president. ➔ Neal's staff found out about the president's abuse of a schoolgirl | – we neither know what he exactly looks like nor his name, age, marital status, we only see him from the distance when he meets an Albanian little girl at the airport (ch. 10, 42:40 – 43:12 ) and from behind when he listens to Motss' "corny speech" (ch. 13, 55:12 – 55:18) |

| | |
|---|---|
| 2. ch. 4, 10:30: Neal comments on the allegations against the president and wants him to comment on them and to return to the US to "face the music"<br>3. ch. 11, 45:23: he declares that the war is over and wants the president to comment on the charges that have been brought up against him, namely the abuse of a schoolgirl<br>4. ch. 17, 01:15:17 – 01:15:35: he wants the president to produce Schumann and suspects fraud when he calls the absence of the flight tardy and says that the president has broken a number of promises<br>- a man in his early 50s, seeming inexperienced in the campaign business, e.g. ch. 4, 10:55 he says the wrong number of days left to election day. breaks off in the middle of the sentence which leaves a bad impression and lets him look unprepared for the interview<br>- fights a "personal" campaign accusing the president of breaking promises, being dishonest and running away from problems ("face the music") | - relies on his PR team, which not only seems to run the country but to "run" the president, they tell him what to do, where to be (where to land in the case of the Albanian little girl) and what to say (they make him hold the speech even though he thinks it's corny)<br>- the only own wish he can realize is a kitten in the TV spot about the war in Albania<br>- his superior position to Ames and Brean makes him look weak lacking self-confidence<br>- if he has not the power to put through his own ideas against his staff, how can he be a powerful and strong leader putting through the interests of the USA? |

**2** The president looks like a puppet in the hands of his PR-team and not like a strong and confident man who is responsible not only for the USA but for the politics in the whole world due to the USA's great influence worldwide. The USA is a superpower and decisions concerning the USA concern other nations, not only 2nd or 3rd world countries, but also strong nations such as Germany. When there is an economic crisis in the USA, the world market will suffer. If the USA takes up new economic relations with a nation like China, economies in other countries are influenced, either positively because a new market develops or negatively because dealers suffer from cheaper prices in China. Regarding political crises between the USA and another nation, third countries are affected, too because of alliances to the USA or the NATO. Speaking of the latter, the USA is one of the steady members of the NATO and influences world politics massively.

A man who leads a nation as strong and influential as the USA must be strong, smart and self-confident. The president in *Wag the Dog* seems to have none of these skills. His opinion seems to be of no importance, he accepts a fake war with Albania in full knowledge of the possible consequences – as we see at the very end of the movie when there really are acts of war looming between the USA and Albania. When Senator Neal wants him to comment on the events, he doesn't; neither on his longer stay in China, nor on the war with Albania, nor on the whereabouts of William Schumann. Senator Neal seems to be a man who says openly what he thinks, and he seems to be someone who cares about his country. He wants an open and honest president and an open and honest relationship to the voters without any secrets or frauds. He most openly criticizes the president in his election video in chapter 3 of the movie but not for the sexual misconduct but for being dishonest. The president is not too far ahead of Neal in the beginning of the movie (17%), but wins the election in the end even though Neal has tried to stop him by revealing the president's misconduct and ending the war. The viewer gets the impression that Neal is too weak to win against the president's staff, but maybe his own staff was just not good or rather unscrupulous enough to win the election.

The Speech

"My fellow Americans, I thank a merciful God, and I am sure each and every one of us will thank that supreme power, whatever we conceive that power to be, that peace is at hand… that peace is at hand

The threat of nuclear terrorism has been quelled. We are in contact with the Albanian Premier, who assures me, and this government credits his assurances, that his country does not wish us ill, and the threat which we perceived was not of his wish, or of his making.

From whence did it come? Our information states it came from a small group of armed and violent dissidents. But that group has been, in the main, subdued. Now: How did we come by this information? It falls to me to reveal to you the existence of a secret group of warriors. Men, yes, and women, trained and pledged their strength, their skills, and, if called upon, their lives, in the service of their fellow Americans.

A group so secret, its very existence has been known to just a few, and known not by a name, but by a designation number, Three-O-Three. A member of the group was left behind what were, then, enemy lines.

And I can only say, to those family members of group 303, whose members are, I know, as I speak, gathering to comfort you, the parents of the missing man, I can only say, no effort will be spared, to find this brave man and to bring him home.

We've just received this photograph of Schumann in captivity, held by a dissident group of Albanian terrorists. Now, I don't know how many of you are familiar with Morse code, but (could you bring the camera closer in here, please...?) You'll see his sweater is worn, it has been unravelled in some places, and those places form dashes and dots. Dashes and Dots. And those dots spell out a message in the Morse code and that message is: "Courage, Mom... Courage, Mom." And he's got the message through: "Courage, Mom..." To the men and women of unit 303, to my fellow citizens I say: "Courage, Mom." I have informed the Albanian government that we will not rest until the safe return of Sergeant Schumann. I'm told his unit mates gave him the nickname, "Old Shoe." Ladies and gentleman, we will not treat him like an Old Shoe, we will not be swayed from every effort to find our Old Shoe.

Thank you, ladies and gentlemen, good night, and God bless."

**a)**

| **Quotation** | **Comment** |
|---|---|
| My fellow Americans | symbol – phrase used first by Kennedy in his inaugural address 1961, reference to president who brought peace/ pacification in the Cold War) |
| God, | |
| that peace is at hand... that peace is at hand | (repetition – emphasis) |
| Men, yes, and women, trained and pledged their strength, their skills, and, if called upon, their lives in the service of their fellow Americans. | (climax – strength, skills in combat and ultimately their lives)<br><br>(parallelism – reference to first paragraph and first words of the speech). |
| "its very existence has been known to just a few, and known not by a name, ..." | (repetition – emphasis) |
| Three-O-Three | (repetition – emphasis) |
| gathering to comfort you, the parents of the missing man, I can only say, no effort will be spared, to find this brave man | (climax and repetition – emphasis on Schumann's situation and focus on him as in individual) |
| ... those places form dashes and dots. Dashes and Dots. | (repetition – emphasis) |
| "Courage, Mom... Courage, Mom." And he's got the message through: "Courage, Mom..." To the men and women of unit 303, to my fellow citizens I say: "Courage, Mom." | (repetition – emphasis) |
| "Old Shoe." Ladies and gentleman, we will not treat him like an Old Shoe, we will not be swayed from every effort to find our Old Shoe. | (repetition – emphasis) |
| Thank you, ladies and gentlemen, good night, and God bless. | (repetition – emphasis)<br>(parallelism – reference to first paragraph and first words of the speech). |

**b)** Individual answers. The student should show awareness of the fact that the speech is well written to not only convince the listener that there really is a soldier missing in combat but also to distract the listener from the fact that the war with Albania might be a fraud. The president apologizes for the secrecy justifying it with the necessity to guarantee the safety of the soldiers in combat. He addresses all Americans, men and women, of all religions united in the hope that the one soldier still missing will return home safely. The president – or rather Motss, the author of the speech – works with the stylistic devices of parallelism and repetition to emphasize and support certain aspects. He repeats the phrase "peace is at hand" to engrave it into the listener's mind that there is no fighting action anymore. He then uses a climax to characterize the men of unit 303 as brave soldiers who would even die in combat for the protection of their "fellow Americans", the American nation. Unit 303 is mentioned four times, not only to remind the listener that it is this unit who has saved the world from the nuclear threat but also to convince him that there really is a unit 303. When the president describes the most important member of the unit, William Schumann, he again uses a climax to emphasize his bravery. The president then appeals to the emotions of the listener when he shows them a photograph of Schumann wearing a torn sweater which allegedly spells "Courage, Mom." in Morse code – of course this photo was probably manipulated by Motss' team. The term "Courage, Mom." is repeated three times, again to carve it into the listener's mind and to appeal to the mother's among the listeners. The secretaries who listened to the speech first were crying at the end, consequently this emotional appeal has worked quite well. Furthermore, not only the emotional level of the listener is addressed, but also the personal one. Everybody can imagine how it feels when a friend or family member is missing and that the relatives are suffering. The president treats the listeners – the American citizens – like relatives when he assures them that he will do everything to bring William Schumann home. He speaks of Schumann as a friend or comrade naming him "our Old Shoe" who will not be forgotten but saved. In the concluding paragraph of the speech he again refers to the American citizens as listeners when he calls them "ladies and gentlemen" twice. It sounds like a reprimand not to forget about Schumann. He closes his speech with the words "God bless" and thus makes the speech look like a sermon, admonishing the Americans to stand together for the salvation of William Schumann.

**4** Individual answers. The students should however note that the talk-show hostess' statement is a conclusion of the discussion with two experts on campaign ads. One of the experts is of the opinion that the "Never change horses…" commercials of the president were the reason for his re-election because they advertised the president's status and reminded the viewer of the fact that the president is responsible for the country and that a change of this position would cause instability and insecurity. The war with Albania had nothing to do with the re-election; the recurring message not to change horses in mid-stream convinced the voters that the present situation is the best for them and the country and shouldn't be changed.

Barack Obama gave the US the feeling of security and peace, even though his election for president meant "a change of horses" (although not in mid-stream, since Bush could not have been re-elected). He not only wanted to end the war with Afghanistan and close Guantanamo but also wanted to stabilize society by supporting the poor and guaranteeing health insurance for every American citizen. On October 9th, 2009 Obama was announced as the winner of the Nobel Peace Prize for "his extraordinary efforts to strengthen international diplomacy and co-operation between peoples".

The committee highlighted Obama's efforts to support international bodies and promote nuclear disarmament. The world has to support what Obama is trying to achieve and help him with his efforts to pacify the world. Only because of the successful campaign in 2008 with well-made commercials, extraordinary speeches that were compared to Kennedy's or even Lincoln's could Obama get this far. He is a charismatic president, but without his campaign staff who knew what sells well and what kind of speech reaches the most voters, he probably wouldn't have won the election.

That he is a product that can be used for advertisement matters is shown by his trip to Denmark to support Chicago's (his hometown) application for the 2016 Olympic Games. No other president has done anything like this before. Even though Obama didn't speak as the president of the USA but as a former citizen of Chicago, there is no doubt that he used his "pop star" status as a president to positively influence the Olympic Committee.

By far not every president or leader of a country has this charisma, but some, such as Obama, Kennedy (and possibly Blair, Sarkozy, ...) are charismatic, good-looking and powerful men who are liked by the voters and the media. They "sell" themselves well – not only their political achievements but also their private lives are of interest for the voters and even for other countries. Tabloids all over the world report about Obama's new dog and Sarkozy's wedding to Carla Bruni, a former top model. The answer to the question whether the president is a product seems to be: certain presidents can become products if they sell themselves well, but certainly not all.

## Worksheet 23: Writing a Review

### Didaktische Anmerkungen

Die SuS schreiben einen *Review* über den Film. Hierbei müssen sie ihr Wissen über die Filmhandlung einbringen und üben noch einmal die strukturierte Gestaltung eines Textes.

### Aufgaben

Write a review about the movie making clear, why you think it is a good or bad movie.

### Lösungen

Individual answers. The student should follow the guidelines how a review should be written. They should also note that *Wag the Dog* is a satire about American politics and the relationship between politics and mass-market entertainment and that media seems to manipulate and thus control politics. They should also take the line "Why does a dog wag its tail? Because the dog is smarter than the tail. If the tail was smarter, it would wag the dog." from the beginning of the movie into consideration and explain who might be the dog and the tail.

The movie is a satire; this genre should also be explained by the students: it mocks real events – sexual abuse in the White House – and makes the president look helpless and absolutely dependent on his PR-staff and as if he is not able to save the election himself.

# Module III Swing Vote

## **Szenenprotokoll** (Gesamtlänge: 115 min., 11 Kapitel)

| | | |
|---|---|---|
| 1 | Town of Texico is shown in the early morning of election day, then change of scenery: in Bud Johnson's home, his daughter is making breakfast, on the radio news about the election day. Relationship between Molly, an about 10-year-old girl, and Bud, her father, as an unusual father-daughter relationship becomes clear. Bud takes Molly to school; they have a discussion about voting and the election. While Molly sees it as a citizen's duty to vote, Bud has no political opinion at all.<br>After having Molly dropped off at school Bud drives to work, he works in an egg farm which employs more Hispanics than Americans.<br>President and his PR manager are talking about the election in the Oval Office, the campaign is not going well at all.<br>President's opponent Greanleaf is campaigning, pleading with his listeners to vote for him and his White House for everybody. Campaign manager is being interviewed; it becomes clear that neither president nor opponent is significantly ahead of the other.<br>Molly reads out her essay about voting in front of her class and because it is so good it will be shown on TV. | 00:00 – 12:53 |
| 2 | Bud is being interviewed by his boss who tells him that he's always late or sick and that he has to fire him. He shows Bud a video in which Bud can be seen drinking liquor and tearing down a huge pile of eggs at work.<br>Molly is waiting for her father in front of the polling station. Bud is playing pool and drinking with his friends and only when he sees Molly on TV does he remember that he promised her to meet her. He runs out of the billiard place but because he's so drunk hits his head on the sign "Vote today" and falls asleep in his car in the parking lot.<br>Molly is angry that her father doesn't show up. In an unnoticed moment she goes to the electoral register, signs in for Bud, gets his ballot and gets into the cabin wanting to vote. While she is putting it into the computer, the cleaning lady pulls the plug and the computer shuts down. Molly runs away and when the cleaning lady has put the plug back in, the computer reports an error.<br>Molly finds Bud in the car and drives him home in his car. Molly is very disappointed and tells Bud that she wants to live with her mother. | 12:54 – 20:15 |
| 3 | Kate Madison, a local reporter, gets a call from the New Mexico voting office asking her if she has voted. On TV is a discussion about the election stating that whoever wins New Mexico wins the election – New Mexico is a swing state and Curry county will be the one to decide the election.<br>Bud and Molly get visitors in the night. They think they are from child services. Bud is afraid that they take Molly away from him due to his drinking and lack of care for his daughter. The men are from the local voting office and after some misunderstandings find out that Bud's vote didn't count and that he has to recast his ballot.<br>Bud is angry with Molly about the trouble she got him into, that he's the one to decide the election.<br>The campaign managers of the president and the opponent organize what has to be done now: go to Texico and find the person who still has to vote.<br>Bud and Molly are fishing and they talk about Molly's mother who for some reason can't be with them. After he has taken Molly to school Bud goes back home and is met by Kate Madison, who has found out that Bud was the one who didn't vote and has to recast his vote. Kate Madison sees this as her chance to finally become a famous reporter/ star on TV. | 20:16 – 34:15 |

| | | |
|---|---|---|
| 4 | Kate Madison has made it: she presents Bud Johnson as the swing voter on TV and causes thousands of journalists to come to Texico to beset Bud's and Molly's trailer home. Molly and Bud discuss what to do and decide to lie and pull through with the recasting of the vote.<br>Texico becomes "campaign ground", every single TV station, newspaper and NPO goes to Texico, and the president and his opponent arrive.<br>The campaign managers have decided to campaign for one man only and they plan to win Bud over. They think it will be quite easy. | |
| 5 | Kate Madison's boss wants her to use Molly to get an interview with Bud.<br>Bud and Molly are constantly on TV and have a security guard now to protect them from too much hassle.<br>Richard Petty, a famous rally driver, shows up in front of Bud's house and wants him to meet a friend of his, who turns out to be the president. While Bud talks to the president, Molly talks to his campaign manager. The president wants to convince Bud to vote for him by telling him that an experienced man has to do the job. He shows Bud the suitcase with the codes for the nuclear missiles. In the course of the conversation it becomes obvious that Bud is very naïve and believes everything the president – and later the opponent – tells him. | |
| 6 | Molly and Bud drive home, Molly tells Bud that he is being bribed by the president and it becomes clear to the viewer that Bud has no idea how great the responsibility is which rests on his shoulders. Through TV Bud is invited to a party thrown by Greenleaf, the president's opponent. Greenleaf's PR manager got Bud's old band together and lets them play – even though some of the members are currently in jail. Kate Madison tries to gain Molly's trust so she can get an exclusive interview with Bud.<br>Both candidates change their political position for Bud's vote, new campaign ads are shot that are only made for Bud. | |
| 7 | Bud gets mail from desperate Americans who seek help from him through his decision. Molly answers the letters in Bud's name; Bud doesn't yet know that they even exist; instead he plays cards with the president. Bud constantly ridicules himself on TV with vague and supposedly funny answers to serious questions. In one interview he even has to be taken off screen because he is makes racist comments about his Mexican co-workers.<br>Kate Madison interviews Bud and it becomes obvious that he doesn't have any political knowledge at all – e.g. he has never heard of the pro-life movement. | |
| 8 | Bud has a fight with Molly and goes to his favourite bar in Texico to meet his friends. He realizes that even his friends don't take him seriously anymore and make fun of his lack of political intelligence as does a talk-show host on TV.<br>Greenleaf doesn't want to completely change his political direction only for Bud but is convinced by his PR manager that only this will let him win the election. The president feels the same and, too, is convinced by his PR manager to proceed with this campaign for one voter.<br>Molly convinces Bud that there should be a debate between the candidates.<br>Again Bud disappoints Molly by forgetting the important day in school when the pupils are allowed to bring their fathers to tell about their job. Moll cries in front of the class and hides the embarrassing fact that her father has forgotten about the appointment by telling the class that he is too busy making his decision to come to school. | |

| | | |
|---|---|---|
| 9 | Sad and disappointed, Molly goes to Kate Madison to tell her about what really happened on election night. When Kate Madison is answering the phone Molly finds a camera hidden under a tablecloth to tape their conversation and leaves Kate Madison's house. She asks her friend Jed to take her to her mum in the evening.<br>When Bud finds out that Molly has run away he is worried and sad that even the secret service officer knows more about his daughter than he does. He rescues Molly from a terrible and emotionally painful encounter with her mother and takes her home.<br>Having found out that Bud didn't vote on election night and since she has a guilty conscience because she wanted to deceive Molly, Kate Madison offers to help Bud with his preparation for the debate. | |
| 10 | The debate starts with a speech from Bud in which he apologizes for his behaviour during the previous week. The viewer only hears the first question of the debate, not more. | |
| 11 | Bud goes to the ballot; again, the viewer is left to guess who will become the president of the United States at the end of the movie. | |

## Zusammenfassung der Filmhandlung

*Swing-Vote* handelt von der unwahrscheinlichen und bislang nur einmal in der Geschichte der USA vorgekommenen Situation, dass die Stimme eines einzelnen Bürgers über die Präsidentschaftswahl entscheidet. Bud Johnson, ein einfacher Arbeiter aus Texico, New Mexico, alleinerziehend und Bewohner eines Trailer-Homes, interessiert sich nur für Bier, Billardspielen und seine Tochter Molly, nicht aber für Fragen der Landespolitik. Molly, eine sehr engagierte Schülerin, möchte ihren Vater davon überzeugen, dass ein Interesse für Politik notwendig und wichtig ist und kann ihn sogar davon überzeugen wählen zu gehen. Bud schafft es aber nicht zum Wahllokal, er war zu betrunken. Molly beschließt nun selbst heimlich zu wählen, was ihr nur dank der Unachtsamkeit einer Putzfrau nicht vollständig gelingt. Der Computerfehler – die Putzfrau hatte aus Versehen den Stecker herausgezogen – wird registriert und Bud muss noch einmal wählen, haben doch der Präsident Boone (Kelsey Grammer) und sein Herausforderer Greenleaf (Dennis Hopper) bislang genau gleich viele Stimmen erhalten. Als die Kandidaten erfahren, wessen Stimme über Sieg oder Niederlage entscheidet, schneiden sie ihre Kampagnen voll und ganz auf Bud Johnson zu, hier wird der Film stellenweise sehr kurzweilig und die Botschaft des Films wird klar: im Wahlkampf geht es irgendwann nicht mehr um Inhalte, sondern um Wählerstimmen und ums Gewinnen.

*Swing-Vote* ist keine Satire; dazu ist die Kritik nicht tiefgründig genug. An keiner Stelle wird das Verhalten der Kandidaten in Frage gestellt oder kritisiert und das Ende mutet sogar als Flucht an, denn der Zuschauer wird den Ausgang der Wahl nie erfahren.

# 1. Pre-viewing Activities

## Worksheet 24: Interpretation of Film Poster and Title

### Didaktische Anmerkungen

Die Analyse dieses Films (WS 1 und 2) wird genauso begonnen wie die von *Wag the Dog*, um den SuS den Einstieg zu erleichtern.

### Aufgaben

**1** *Jot down your first thoughts about the title and the poster of the movie.*

**2** *Write in ONE short sentence on your flashcard what you think the movie might be about and put your flashcard on the board.*

### Lösungen

**1** Individuelle Antworten, die aber folgende Aspekte enthalten sollten:
Title: A vote that can swing the outcome of an election one way or the other because the voter has no allegiance to any political party and whose unpredictable decisions
Poster: "A nobody becomes the voice of everybody." Kevin Costner has the leading role, little girl probably his daughter, they have to face an important decision that influences the whole nation.

**2** individuelle Antworten

## Worksheet 25: The Trailer

### Aufgaben

**1** *Watch the trailer (twice) on:* http://www.imdb.com/video/imdb/vi2363687193/. *Answer the following questions:*

**a)** *What is the plot of the movie about?* **b)** *Where does it take place?* **c)** *Who are the main characters?* **d)** *Write a short summary of the movie with just the information from the trailer as a basis.*

### Lösungen

**a)** Bud Johnson's vote in the presidential election didn't count due to a computer problem. He has to recast his vote and his single vote will decide the election. The president and his opponent try to convince Johnson to vote for them. Bud Johnson's daughter Molly seems to play an important role concerning her father's decision.

**b)** Rural America

**c)** Kevin Costner, Nathan Lane, Kelsey Grammar, Dennis Hopper, Madeleine Caroll.

**d)** Durch die Länge des Trailers von 2,30 Minuten wird schon viel über den Inhalt des Filmes verraten. Die SuS wissen, dass beide Kandidaten Bud Johnsons Stimme haben wollen, um Präsident der Vereinigten Staaten zu werden bzw. zu bleiben. Die Beschreibung der Art und Weise, wie diese Überzeugung des wichtigsten Wählers vonstatten gehen soll, kann von den SuS jedoch kreativ erarbeitet werden, ebenso die spezielle Beziehung zwischen Molly und Bud, die im Trailer nur angedeutet wird.

## 2. While-viewing Activities

### Worksheet 26: Characters and Characterisation

**Didaktische Anmerkungen**

Die SuS charakterisieren Molly und Bud anhand der ersten beiden Kapitel des Films und untersuchen ihre unterschiedliche politische Einstellung. Außerdem sollen sie ihre eigene Einstellung zur Teilnahme an Wahlen darstellen.

**Aufgaben**

**1** *Watch the first two chapters of the movie and describe the characters of Bud and Molly.*

**2** *Describe Molly's and Bud's political attitudes.*

**3** *What do you think about voting? Give reasons for your opinion.*

**Lösungen**

**1 Bud**

| | |
|---|---|
| outward appearance | scruffy, untended single father in his 40s |
| behaviour, words and thoughts | • lazy, doesn't want to get up,<br>• undisciplined, wants Molly to skip school because he's too tired to get up<br>• drinks too much beer, loses his job due to his drinking problem, not having shown up on time at his job and having too many sick certificates; doesn't fight for his job but resigns<br>• works on an egg farm, doesn't have enough money to pay for the phone bill or repair of the heater<br>• only knows little about Molly's life, doesn't know her friends or her teacher's name<br>• behaves in a clumsy way around people of better education<br>• wants to protect his daughter and his belongings from others<br>• can be influenced easily by gifts, he doesn't realize how serious his situation is |
| others' reactions | • his friends, neighbours and the TV hosts think he's stupid and ignorant about the great responsibility he has<br>• the president sees quickly that Bud is not smart enough to understand the way politics are played and thus he plays with him (ch. 5: 51:00) to get his vote: eating ice-cream, playing football. |
| feelings and attitudes | • loves his daughter unconditionally, would do anything for her, is always afraid she might be taken away from him due to his unstable lifestyle<br>• doesn't want to take a stand, neither in his job nor in the election |

**Molly**

| | |
|---|---|
| outward appearance | pretty young girl, about 10 years old |
| behaviour, words and thoughts | • doesn't behave like a little girl but like a grown woman towards her father, rails at him when he doesn't get up<br>• calls him Bud, not Dad<br>• very self-confident when she talks to adults, she is not afraid of the campaign managers of the candidates but sees them for what they are<br>• she is the only one who sees the bribes with which the candidates try to get Bud's vote |
| others' reactions | admiration due to her cleverness (Ms. Madison, president's PR manager) |

| | |
|---|---|
| feelings and attitudes | • loves her father even though he drinks and forgets things<br>• self-confident and smart<br>• misses her mother, has a break-down after her father has disappointed again |

**2** Bud doesn't believe in voting; he has the feeling that his vote doesn't count anyway. He is of the opinion that the politicians only want to make the voters think they are in control, even though they aren't. No mater who you vote for, he doesn't have a health insurance and has to sell his blood when Molly gets sick.

Molly wants him to vote because she has learned from Mrs. Abernathy, her teacher that it is a social contract and you have to vote. She even registered her father to vote.

**3** individual answers

## Worksheet 27: A Letter to Bud

### Didaktische Anmerkungen

Die Methode des *„Letter-writing"* ist ein wichtiger Bestandteil des Englischunterrichts geworden. Die SuS sollen in die Rolle der Wahlkandidaten schlüpfen und in einem Brief an Bud Johnson Versprechen formulieren, um ihn zur Stimmabgabe motivieren.

### Aufgaben

*Watch the movie up to chapter 5. Imagine you were one of the candidates and had the opportunity to write one letter to Bud to convince him to vote for you. Write the letter.*

### Lösungen

Individual answers. The task seems easier than it is, though. The students have to go back to Module 1 and the party programs of the Democrats and the Republicans. Then they have to think of the topics Bud Johnson might be interested in. The following examples are possible: "insourcing" is a problem for him, so they should tell him that they'll make sure no more foreigners will be employed and steal his job (Greenleaf has to change his party program in this case). He doesn't have a health insurance and has to donate his blood in case Molly gets sick, so they should offer him an affordable health insurance (here Boone has to change his position).

## Worksheet 28: The Campaign Managers

### Didaktische Anmerkungen

Den SuS werden die Kapitel gezeigt, in denen die Wahlkampfmanager der beiden Kandidaten auftreten. Die SuS sollen sich Notizen zu den Charakteren machen und anschließend eine Charakterisierung anhand des bereits bekannten Worksheets aus Modul 2 ausarbeiten.

Als vorbereitende Hausaufgabe sollen die SuS sich mit den Wahlkampfversprechen von Barack Obama beschäftigen. Welche wurden gehalten, welche nicht, an welchen wird noch gearbeitet? Man sollte die Lerngruppe aufgrund des Umfangs des Arbeitsauftrages aufteilen. In der Folgestunde wird die Debatte der beiden Kandidaten am Ende des Films thematisiert werden und die SuS sollen Fragen formulieren, die sie den Kandidaten gestellt hätten, wären sie in Bud's Position gewesen.

### Aufgaben

**1** *Describe the characters of the president's and Greenleaf's campaign managers.*

**2** *"The campaign managers in* Swing Vote *bear a resemblance to Conrad Brean from* Wag the Dog. *" Comment on this statement.*

### Lösungen

**1** Individual answers. Both men are eager to win; Fox because he's used to winning and Crumb because he has not won any election in his job as a campaign manager yet. They are both willing to bend the law as far as possible to get that final vote. Not only Fox would be willing to sell his mother's soul as Molly has read in the paper to win the election. Both feel superior to the candidates / their employees who have strange ideas about their first encounter with Johnson, such as eating ice-cream (Boone). Crumb and Fox are able to convince the candidates of anything, even neglecting their principles. They tell them that winning is the only thing that matters an one has to only work for that, principles that are not helping to win Bud's vote need to be forgotten about. Boone and Greenleaf seem to be strong men with strong wills who have great problems with a campaign for a person like Bud. Still they listen to their campaign managers to win.

| **Relevant excerpts from the movie** | |
|---|---|
| ch 1 (7:56) | The president's managaer, Martin Fox: pushes the campaign by sending the "correct" voters to the poles and increasing certain TV spots to influence the voters |
| ch 1 (10:14) | Greenleaf's manager, Art Crumb: skilfully taunts the president and his campaign in his interview ("This is operation real deal.") and spreads new rumours which he envelopes in supposedly inoffensive statements. |
| ch 3 (27:45) | Crumb/ Fox: both planning a war, even if the methods of winning are illegal, their strategies are quite similar |
| ch 4 (40:52) | Crumb convincing Greenleaf that a one-man-campaign is no problem and that they are going to win, even though he doesn't know how to do it, Fox follows the exact same strategy in wanting Bud and the candidates meet. |
| ch 5 (47:39) | Fox, greeting Bud and Molly in Airforce One, constantly telling Bud what to do and to say, he doesn't take Bud seriously thinking he's just some white-trash-trailer-park-guy. He doesn't take Molly seriously either and is amazed about her smartness. |
| ch 6/ 7 (56:00) | Crumb behaving arrogantly towards Molly and Bud, he arranged everything the way he hopes Bud likes it, even getting his band out of prison. He obviously has told Greenleaf how to behave and what to do, e.g. has fishing vocabulary ready for Greenleaf when he needs it in a conversation with Bud. |
| (1:07); (1:15) | Fox has his spies at the party and reacts immediately: the president becomes an environmental protector even though his party is known for supporting great energy companies = the first policy reversal. Crumb also reacts immediately and throws the party program overboard, the vote is more important than the parties' principles for both men. |

| | |
|---|---|
| ch.8 (1:21) | it becomes obvious that Crumb desperately wants to win the election because he has never won any election/ campaign he has worked on. He only cares about principles if they make him win the election. Fox even wants the president to offer Bud a job (1:23), even though he doesn't seem to be qualified for anything. |

**2** Individual answers. There is a resemblance because Fox and Crumb manipulate the candidates as much as Brean manipulates the president in playing along with his "campaign". All three men are self-confident, know how to handle the media, know what to say in interviews and how to bend the truth. They are all at war during the campaign, Brean needing the great majority of the voters for the re-electon of the president, Crumb and Fox needing only one vote.

## Worksheet 29: Bud's Speech

### Didaktische Anmerkungen

Die SuS formulieren Fragen, die für sie im Wahlkampf von Interesse gewesen wären und ihre persönlich Wahlentscheidung beeinflusst hätten. Die Lehrkraft sollte die Fragen nicht bewerten, sondern alle Fragen unkommentiert zur Diskussion stellen. In der zweiten Aufgabe analysieren die SuS Buds Rede vor Beginn der Debatte.

### Aufgaben

**1** *Taking into consideration what you have found out about Barack Obama's promises in the campaign 2008, which questions would you think are of major interest in a debate and could influence a swing voter's decision? Write them on a flash card and put them on the board.*

**2** *Analyse Bud's speech before the debate, ch.10 (1:44) paying special attention to the use of stylistic devices.*

**3** *Comment on the speech.*

### Lösungen

**1** Individual answers. Examples of problematic issues are the health insurance, shutting down Guantanamo, amd the national debt.

**2** "Mr. President, Mr. Greenleaf, I'd like to thank you for your hospitality, it has ben really interesting. I said a lot of things I didn't mean and you both made a lot of promises (repetition: emphasis) you probably won't be able to keep (here Bud skilfully avoids accusing the candidates of lying to him or bribing him to get his vote). To be honest, the last ten days have felt like a weird dream. But what was once funny isn't anymore. And after what I've read I've scared the hell out of America. I know that the world is watching, maybe even laughing. People on my own TV are saying that America somehow deserves this moment. I guess that means me (symbol: he is important and negative/ dangerous for America). I can't say that I've been much of anything most of my life. It's sort of like somewhere along the way I checked out (figurative speech). And it's not like I didn't have big dreams to begin with but I had something once, something close to faith or hope or whatever words you want to use for how good life could be. But then the years they start moving quicker and all of a sudden what's going good out there for everybody else is not so good for you. But tonight I feel embarrassed. I've had my chances more than most. I've grown up in a country where if I had decided to do more with my life than just drift and drink (alliteration) then I could be standing where maybe you stand tonight. Instead I've taken freely and I've given (contradiction/opposite: give and take as a balance of things, Bud hasn't cared about this balance) nothing. I'm ashamed in front of my daughter and my country (climax). I've never served or sacrificed (alliteration and climax referring to the military, the "duty" to your country), the only heavy lifting I've ever been asked is simple stuff like, you know, pay attention, vote (paradoxon, voting isn't simple stuff but an important achievement of a democracy). If America has a true enemy tonight, I guess it's me (symbol: if Bud doesn't take his responsibility seriously he is not only a threat to America but to the world). Tonight a below-average man is going to choose between two exceptional men (contrast). Tomorrow one man's vote is going to make a difference. Because tomorrow we're going to have a president and not just someone to fill a chair in Washington.We need someone who is bigger than their speeches. The kind of president we learned about in school when we still cared. America needs a big thinker, you know, like a giant (climax), really. Someone who has the guts to get in front of our problems (symbol/ figurative speech: president will protect America against dangers), somebody who has the wisdom to lead us to a place where we are at peace with ourselves and the world (symbol/ figurative speech: biblical reference: Moses led Israel into the Promised Land). And just for the record, I want you both to know that I think a hell a lot of you."

**3** Individual answers. The students should note that Bud has changed from a negligent drunk to a "responsible citizen" of the USA, a change that is fairly unlikely to happen within 10 days. While "Wag the Dog" is a political satire, "Swing Vote" isn't, it's just a comedy about a man who all of a sudden becomes the most important citizen of the US. Just because Molly runs away from home, Bud's character is not going to change from a corrupt child in adult's clothes to a responsible, critical, humble and mature man.

## 3. Post-viewing Activities

### Worksheet 30: Radio Interview

#### Didaktische Anmerkungen

Die SuS hören einen Ausschnitt aus einer Sendung des National Public Radio als Hörverstehensübung. Es handelt sich um ein Interview mit Kevin Costner am 27.07.2008 über den Film *Swing Vote*.

Nachdem das Interview den SuS einmal vorgespielt wurde, erhalten sie ein Arbeitsblatt und hören das Interview erst dann zum zweiten Mal. Die SuS sollen insbesondere zur politischen Aussagekraft des Films Stellung nehmen. Teilweise können die Arbeitsaufträge des Arbeitsblattes auch als Hausaufgabe aufgegeben werden. Ein Download von diesem Interview findet man unter: *http://www.npr.org/templates/story/story.php?storyId=92976013* (Gesamtlänge: 6:29)

**Aufgaben**

Listen to the interview and try to understand as much as you can.

1 *What is the purpose of the interview?*

2 *What's the atmosphere between Costner and the radio show host like?*

3 *How does Costner handle the host's criticism concerning the movie?*

4 *Comment on the host's statement: "Now I have to say, though, that as we're talking about both sides being represented as being pretty flimsy, in the end, it does seem like the correct stand on the issues in this movie is pretty left of center".*

**Lösungen**

1 Promoting the movie Swing Vote and Kevin Costner's new CD.

2 Costner tries to get around certain answers. He doesn't want to comment on his political position and how it might have been reflected in the movie, the host is not able to nail him to get the information he wants. When she realizes that she decides to talk about his musical efforts with his new band.

3 He admits that the film is a comedy and not meant as a critical movie about politics. He refuses to accept the criticism that he missed the chance to ask uncomfortable questions or mention uncomfortable issues in more detail. He mentions the problems of the working poor such as job insecurity and lack of health insurance but he doesn't offer any solution to the problem. In the second half of the movie these issues aren't even talked about any longer. Costner didn't want to make a political movie but a comedy about politics and succeeded in doing so. His great times as a critical actor as in "13 Days" and "JFK" seem to be long gone.

4 Individual answers. The students should observe, though, that the movie doesn't take any political position. It is a comedy, as Costner says in the interview, and nothing more. If the movie was meant to be a political satire it would be more critical about the problems for America's working poor. The only criticism of the current government occurs in chapter 1, when Bud takes Molly to school and she tells him that the two party system is not taking care of the problems of the working poor and thus Bud should be independent politically (ch 1, 5:05): "Because the two party system has neglected the needs of the working poor."). Problems like unaffordable health insurance and job insecurity due to competition of Hispanic emloyees who accept lower wages are only briefly mentioned (ch 1 when Bud says that in case Molly gets sick he has to sell his blood to pay for the doctor's bills and ch 2 when he is fired) and not further discussed. If Bud was a politically responsible citizen he would have asked the candidates to take a position on these issues. The only chance the movie has to discuss these problems and to take a position is in chapter 11 when Bud asks his first question to the candidates which is from a working poor asking the candidates how it could be that in the richest country in the world so many people can barely afford to live here (ch 11, 01:49:06). But instead of taking this chance and getting into more detail, the scene ends and we see Bud go to the ballot, casting his vote. It might be unsatisfying for the viewer not to know who Bud voted for. But again, politics are not of interest here, but Bud's transformation from a politically ignorant drunk to a responsible citizen of the USA, obeying the "social contract" of voting, as Costner says in the interview

("I thought what happened at the end was that Bud, instead of doing a rah-rah speech, he looked at himself, and he dug really deep, you know, and ultimately, he said, you know, an average man is going to pick between two exceptional men. Does that seem fair? Not really, but that's what it's wound itself down to."). Whether or not this transformation in just 10 days is realistic is questionable.

**Interview Text**
**Kevin Costner on Swing Vote on NPR on July 27, 2008**

ANDREA SEABROOK, host:
Now the story of a guy who's wooed by two of the most powerful men on earth. One night, Bud Johnson is shaken awake by his young daughter. He opens his door to this.

*(Soundbite of crowd of people)*

SEABROOK: The flashing bulbs and media frenzy of a political firestorm. It turns out Bud is the swing voter, and everybody wants a piece of him. Kevin Costner plays Bud in the new movie, "Swing Vote," which opens this Friday. Kevin Costner, thanks so much for coming in.

Mr. KEVIN COSTNER (Actor): Well thanks.

SEABROOK: So Bud, he ends up being the one guy whose vote the entire election turns on. It's really circumstances that make the Florida recount in 2000 look tame.

Mr. COSTNER: Yeah, both – what happens is it does come down a single vote, and no one's sure how it's been cast. There's been a voter error. Legally, you had to have 10 days for this individual to recast his vote, and so what happens if you have Kelsey Grammer playing the Republican president and…

SEABROOK: Dennis Hopper.

Mr. COSTNER: Dennis Hopper is playing the Democratic candidate running for the office. If you've got two men vying for the biggest job on the planet, is it any wonder that maybe when their base is reduced to one that they begin to waffle?

SEABROOK: Yeah, there are these fantastic little – I mean, a really bright spot in the movie are the parodies of political ads that these two make to try and get Bud's vote.

Mr. COSTNER: And at the same time separating themselves completely 180 degrees from what they really believe.

*(Soundbite of film, "Swing Vote")*

*(Soundbite of music)*

Mr. KELSEY GRAMMER (Actor): (As President Andrew Boone): Bud, with your help, this Republican administration will say I do to gay marriage.

Unidentified Man (Actor): (As character) I do.

Unidentified Woman (Actor): (As character) I do.

SEABROOK: The Democratic candidate makes an anti-abortion rights and a pro-life and…

Mr. COSTNER: And immigration. I mean, people are just running across the border.

SEABROOK: Right, yeah. That one was very funny. Now I have to say, though, that as we're talking about both sides being represented as being pretty flimsy, in the end, it does seem like the correct stand on the issues in this movie is pretty left of center.

Mr. COSTNER: I don't know where you're going there, but I'm listening.

SEABROOK: Okay, for example the working poor. The issues that really seem to coalesce as the issues to be worked on in this country are about the working poor, health insurance, jobs. There isn't really much talk about bloated government, taxes the sort of social conservative agenda, other than the farcical commercial on gay marriage.

Mr. COSTNER: Well, we couldn't take on the whole issue. I mean, this isn't "Thirteen Days."

SEABROOK: Sure.

Mr. COSTNER: It's not "JFK." It's a comedy, and ultimately, those issues I don't see as being left or right. That's what always bothered me about (unintelligible). I mean, it seems to me in the country that about 80 percent of our problems are not really problems. They're just problems that exist between people who can't get their ego out of the way in order to solve things for Americans.

SEABROOK: But it seems like the issues you choose and the priorities you put them in, the movie ends up looking like you want people to vote, but you kind of want them to vote for the Democrat.

Mr. COSTNER: I didn't really get that feeling, but – and that's the beauty of a movie. Somebody else got that feeling. I thought what happened at the end was that Bud, instead of doing a rah-rah speech, he looked at himself, and he dug really deep, you know, and ultimately, he said, you know, an average man is going to pick between two exceptional men. Does that seem fair? Not really, but that's what it's wound itself down to.

SEABROOK: You portrayed on reporter getting a lot of pressure from her producer, her TV producer back at the station, and there's a line where he says something like this is bigger than God. This is television.

Mr. COSTNER: Yeah, yeah, this isn't news anymore. This is bigger than news. This is television. Listen, I have a lot of friends in the business that you're in, and I can't tell you the writers that have to write about me or interview me or whatever, the pressure they come under once their story is turned in, how it gets re-edited, and they see their story evaporate down to some kind of story that we've, you know, all seen, and when a producer says no, you ask him about his first marriage, you do that, and you go, I don't want to do that, and he goes you do it. The air goes out of the room.

SEABROOK: So tell me about your first marriage – no, I'm just joking.

(*Soundbite of laughter*)

Mr. COSTNER: Gotcha.

(*Soundbite of laughter*)

Mr. COSTNER: You almost didn't have – you couldn't even let it lay there long enough.

SEABROOK: I couldn't help myself.

Mr. COSTNER: Yeah, you couldn't even let it lay there to go beat, beat, beat, that's a joke.

SEABROOK: You're right.

Mr. COSTNER: Beat, beat, beat.

SEABROOK: Beat, beat, beat. Your band, you formed a band called Modern West.

Mr. COSTNER: Yeah.

SEABROOK: And you're coming out with a CD in October.

Mr. COSTNER: I don't want to – I'm not content to just be what people think that I am. Music was a part of my life before movies. I was – in the church, my grandmother was the – played for the choir, my mom was in the choir. I was a wise man as eight years old, you know, and all the Christmas stuff.

*(Soundbite of laughter)*

Mr. COSTNER: So I would sing, "O Holy Night," you know, and all that stuff. I took classical piano. I've, you know, found myself around the world, even doing these press junkets and finding myself in the city and in hotel rooms, and I talk about the movie or whatever, and I don't really have an exchange that I feel comfortable with, and being able to play music, if I was playing tonight in Washington, and you were able, you know, to come see it, I would gather that you would have a different feeling about me. It might be a bad feeling, or it might be a greater feeling, but it would be what I would call an expansion of a relationship, where you go: I know now more about him than I've ever known. So I love being in front of people and telling stories, whether it's in music or in movies.

SEABROOK: Kevin Costner's new movie is called "Swing Vote." Thanks so much for coming in.

Mr. COSTNER: You're welcome.

SEABROOK: We really appreciate it.

*(Soundbite of music)*

# Module IV The War Room

## **Szenenprotokoll** (Gesamtlänge: 92 min., 12 Kapitel)

| | | |
|---|---|---|
| 1-6 | - primaries and campaign up to the debate between Clinton, Bush and Perot<br>- problems of campaign such as rumours about Clinton's affair with a woman and his alleged draft avoidance<br>- Carville and Stephanopoulos shown in their effort to gain votes for Bill Clinton, meetings and conferences, "pep talks" for campaign workers (Carville plays the main part in this, he is a charismatic speaker who can get people's attention) and effort to help Clinton win the election<br>- party conventions with huge audiences waving Clinton signs and Clinton becoming the Democratic presidential candidate<br>- tactics of spin doctors: manipulation of the press, finding soft spots in the opponent's campaign (Bush's banners being printed in Brasil with campaign money)<br>- press conferences and press meetings, Carville soothing down speculations and accusations against Clinton | 00:00 – 57:30 |
| 7-8 | - the presidential debate and its aftermaths, press statements of the campaign officials of Clinton and Bush | 57:31 – 01:07:29 |
| 9-10 | - Carville and Stephanopoulos fighting off final threats to Clinton's triumph such as more affairs of Clinton with other women<br>- final speech from James Carville the night before the election<br>- fear that they might have lost the election in spite of good campaign, atmosphere on election day when the numbers are coming in | 01:07:30 – 01:26:04 |
| 11-12 | - after the election Clinton has won (Clinton calls Stephanopoulos and asks him what he should say) | 01:26:05 – 01:29:38 |

## Zusammenfassung der Filmhandlung

Hauptperson dieses Dokumentarfilms ist nicht, wie man annehmen mag, Bill Clinton, sondern seine beiden Wahlkampfmanager, George Stephanopoulos (*director of communications*) und James Carville (Strategiedirektor). Von der Planungszentrale *The War Room* aus steuerten sie einen Wahlkampf, der vom Sieg Clintons mystifiziert wurde. Der Film zeigt 90 Minuten lang, was im Wahlkampf 1992 alles passiert ist: die Vorwahlen in New Hampshire, Besprechungen, Strategiesitzungen, Angriff und Verteidigung gerade in Bezug auf Clintons ehebrecherischem Verhalten und auch TV-Debatten, die die Gegner Clintons lächerlich erscheinen lassen. Der Film nimmt die Perspektive des Clinton Teams ein und zeigt, wie *spin doctors* wirklich agieren.

## Didaktische Anmerkungen

### 1. Pre-viewing Activities

### Worksheet 31: A Political Documentary

**Aufgaben**

1 *Imagine a presidential candidate asked you to make a documentary about his or her campaign. What would be the most important events you'd include in the documentary? Write your ideas on a flashcard.*

2 *What would be the differences to a movie like* Wag the Dog *or* Swing Vote*? Would the movies have anything in common? Take notes.*

3 *Watch the trailer (twice) on* http://www.imdb.com/video/screenplay/vi1140588825/ *and pay special attention on both events and film techniques Take notes.*

**Lösungen**
**1** Background information (without any scandals) on the presidential nominee, events/ interviews/ newscasts before and after the nomination, work of the campaign team (how the staff is motivated, what needs to be done), presidential debates, events after the election, first days as the new president or the one who lost the election

**2** Differences: no actors, no background music, no screenplay but authentic film material about the nominee and his team, maybe different use of cinematic devices
Similarities: "drama" or thrill of campaign, suspense, scandals (affairs, lies...) and a happy ending

**3** The film is about Bill Clinton's campaign 1992 from the perspective of his campaign staff. (James Carville – campaign manager – and George Stephanopoulos – director of communications). The work of the campaign staff is shown, meetings, press interviews and statements of the opponent and his campaign staff. They have to fight off attacks from opponents and the outcome of scandals (people having torn down Clinton's campaign posters, Bill Clinton's lover)
As far as the film techniques used are concerned, the main difference to a movie is the use of the hand camera. The pictures are more intense because the camera man gets closer to the "characters" than in a normal movie. The major field sizes are the close-up and the extreme close-up. The camera is almost always in the over-the-shoulder-shot or reverse-angle-shot position and the angle is mostly eye-level shot. These techniques almost turn the documentary into a diary about the campaign.

## 2. While-viewing Activities

### Worksheet 32: A Real Campaign

**Didaktische Anmerkungen**
Die SuS sollen die Unterschiede zwischen dem Dokumentarfilm *The War Room* und den Spielfilmen *Wag the Dog* und *Swing Vote* herausarbeiten, wobei der Schwerpunkt auf den Figuren der Wahlkampfmanager, den sogenannten *spin doctors*, liegt. Im Rückblick auf Modul 1 sollen zunächst die einzelnen Phase des Wahlkampfes notiert werden: die Vorwahlen, die Schlammschlacht während der Kampagne, *Conventions*, Debatten und schließlich die Wahlnacht. In *Wag the Dog* und in *Swing Vote* sind diese Phasen teilweise dargestellt, wichtiger aber ist schon hier die Analyse der Arbeitsweise der Wahlkampfmanager. Wie werden sie mit Problemen fertig? Wie manipulieren sie, auch im richtigen Wahlkampf von 1991, die Medien? Wie ist das Verhältnis zwischen Wahlkampfmanager und Wahlkandidat? Werden die Kandidaten wirklich gesteuert und stellen eigene Ziele in den Hintergrund, nur um zu gewinnen? Diese Fragen sollen im Vergleich der drei Filme beantwortet werden.

**Aufgaben**

**1** *Take notes about the different stages of a real campaign.*

**2** *What are the main problems for the campaign managers and how do they solve them?*

**3** *What is the relationship between the candidate and the campaign manager like? Can you compare it to the relationship as shown in either Wag the Dog or Swing Vote?*

**Lösungen**

**1** Primaries, nomination of the candidates, conventions, debates and the election night.

**2** Individual answers. In the movie the main problems for Clinton or rather Carville and Stephanopoulos occur after the primaries just before the other Democratic candidates resign: accusations against Clinton concerning affairs with various women (eg ch 1, 04:40 – 09:05), accusations that he fled from military service, accusations that he demonstrated against the USA in Moscow and that he financed his campaign with his wife's money.
Concerning the affair with Gennifer Flowers Bill Clinton seems to be able to handle it well himself. Carville then motivates the campaign workers (ch 1 09:30) to fight other accusations and not to believe anything that is said by the Republicans because it was just not true. Stephanopoulos skilfully fights off accusations about Clinton's character admitting that there have been marital problems and avoiding comment on the draft issue (ch 212:46 – 13:21). Carville also is a master of twisting the words especially when it comes to Clinton demonstrating in Moscow. Both men use facts to fight the problems. Carville repeatedly tells journalists that they don't have to believe him, they should take a look at the facts (numbers/ polls) and then they'll be convinced, too. They skilfully manipulate the media by focusing on Clinton's program and avoiding scandals and slinging mud at the other candidates. Carville says that he likes Bush as a politician but doesn't like him as president, for example (ch 3, 21:13–21:22). They don't want to win their campaign by bashing the opponent; but with better and more convincing arguments. They want to win because the voters have the impression that Clinton is the better choice politically. They only attack the opponent politically, never personally, as the Republicans do with Clinton (ch 6, 49:20 posters printed in Brazil with illegally used campaign money). Both men are very self-confident in their work for Clinton. The viewer believes them when they say Clinton is going to win.

**3** Carville and Stephanopoulos work for Clinton and they seem to be convinced of his politics. Both write speeches for Clinton (ch 4 28:37, Stephanopoulos writes Clinton's speech, Carville prepares a speech for him in ch 4, 32:30 – 36:00). Clinton lets them speak for him on TV (ch 2, Stephanopoulos fighting off accusations in a TV interview) and he asks them what to say (ch 11:01:26:52) In the beginning of the movie Clinton is with his campaign team, having coffee, making phone calls and having a good time. The self-confidence of Carville and Stephanopoulos made Clinton strong, their skills as spin doctors of the media and writers of speeches enables Clinton to win the presidency. Carville even practices the losing-speech of Clinton in chapter 10 with a wide smile on his face, just before Stephanopoulos already plans Clinton's winning speech and his first public appearance as the President of the USA (ch 10, 01:23). The relationship of the three men is close and looks like a friendship, albeit a professional one. Clinton even asks Stephanopoulos what to say after he has already won (ch 10, 1:27). This show the deep trust he has in his campaign managers. They didn't manipulate him to become the president, they helped him.

## Worksheet 33: Stephanopoulos und Carville

### Didaktische Anmerkungen

Die SuS analysieren zwei kurze Reden von Stephanopoulos und Carville aus Kapitel 9 des Films. Am Abend des Wahltages erhält Clintons Wahlkampfteam einen vertraulichen Anruf. Stephanopoulos nimmt den Anruf entgegen und es stellt sich heraus, dass jemand aus Perots Wahlkampfteam veröffentlichen möchte, dass Clinton Vater eines unehelichen schwarzen Kindes ist. Stephanopoulos reagiert selbstbewusst und ruhig und es gelingt ihm die Veröffentlichung zu verhindern. Die SuS sollen die Redemittel von Stephanopoulos analysieren. Sie sollten die Rede als Text erhalten, den Filmausschnitt aber auch mehrmals vorgespielt bekommen.

### Aufgaben

*Analyse either Stephanopoulos conversation on the telephone with an unknown person or Carville's speech to the campaign team on election night, paying particular attention to the men's skills as campaign managers.*

### Lösungen

Ch. 9, 01: 08:06 – 01:09:58 (Stephanopoulos):
Stephanopoulos: "Read it to me. I can send you a fax of names, addresses, phone numbers of who you had an affair with. It wouldn't make it true. Yeah … I just… believe me... it has been worked at by every major news organisation. Everything. And it is completely bullshit. If you went on the radio and said that Bill Clinton is the father of an illegitimate black child you would be laughed at. People would think you're crazy. We're not going to lose. We are going to win. He is going to be president. Well, no, don't think of it like that, let's take it at two levels: Number one of course it's not going to matter. But number two: think of yourself. I guarantee you that if you do this you'll never work in democratic politics again. Maybe you don't want to; I'm not saying that it matters. You'll be embarrassed before the national press corps. People will think… Nobody will believe you and people will think you're scummy. That… the alternative is: you don't do it, it causes you some temperate pain with people who tomorrow aren't going to matter and you have a campaign that understands that in a difficult time you did something right. Em… you know, that's important. I mean, it doesn't mean anything; we can't do anything for you specifically or anything like that."

Stephanopoulos stays calm and appeals to the caller's common sense. Skilfully he manoeuvres the caller into believing that he or she is lying or the facts he or she wants to unveil are not strong enough to be believed by the public. Stephanopoulos doesn't know whether the caller is lying or indeed telling the truth, after all, Clinton has admitted to having had various affairs. Without threatening the caller or promising money Stephanopoulos cleverly convinces the person not to publish the news that Bill Clinton is the father of an illegitimate black child.

Ch.9 01:11:15 – 01:13:35 (Carville):
Carville: "There's a simple doctrine "Outside of a person's love the most sacred thing that they can give is their labour." And somehow along the way we tend to forget that. And labour is a very precious thing that you have. And anytime that you can combine labour with love you've made a merge. And I think we're going to win tomorrow. And I think that the governor is going to fulfil his promise and change America. And I think many of you are going to go on and help him. I'm a political professional, that's what I do for living, I am proud of it. We changed the way campaigns are run. It used to be... there was a hierarchy. If you were on one floor, you couldn't go to another floor. If you were here on an organisation chart, there was no room for you there (gestures to a higher degree/ floor), everyone was compartmentalized. But you people showed you could be trusted. Everybody in this room, everybody. And if people are going to tell you that you were lucky, deny it. Ben Hogan [a famous golfer] said: "Golf is a game of luck, the more I play, the luckier I get." The harder you work, the luckier you are. I was 33 years old before I went from Washington to New York. With 42 I won my first campaign. And I am happy for all of you. You've been part of something special in my life and I'll never forget what you have done. Thank you."

Carville, even though he was the head of the campaign together with Stephanopoulos, makes himself equal to the other campaign workers saying that there used to be a hierarchy but there isn't anymore. He treats them like family members who could not only be trusted but who mean something to him. He also gives them the advice never to give up working hard; there will be a success, even if it takes some time – for him 9 years. When he holds this speech he is fighting back tears which make the speech even more emotional. Carville really combined love with labour, whether all the other campaign workers did so remains unknown. In this speech Carville shows how deeply involved he was in the campaign, he not only worked hard for Clinton but really wanted to win the campaign himself (possibly because his wife was working for the other side?)

## Worksheet 34: The Debate

### Didaktische Anmerkungen

Die SuS sehen sich die Debatte (oder einen Ausschnitt davon) zwischen Perot, Bush und Clinton vom 15.10.1992 an. Sie notieren sich ihre Eindrücke zu den Kandidaten in Bezug auf deren Überzeugungskraft und Glaubwürdigkeit. Anschließend sollen sie begründen, wen von den drei Kandidaten sie gewählt hätten. Abschließend wird analysiert, warum Clinton laut Umfragen nach der Debatte diese gewonnen hat.

### Aufgaben

*Watch the 2nd presidential debate from 1992 with Ross Perot, George Bush senior and Bill Clinton on* http://www.c-span.org/Watch/Media/1992/10/15/HP/A/10364/1992+Presidential+Town+Hall+Debate.aspx.

**1** *Note down your impressions of the candidates: how do they present themselves? Are they credible?*

**2** *Who would you vote for? Why?*

**3** *Check Carville's and Stephanopoulos's reactions after the debate. How do they react? Was the outcome of the debate successful for Bill Clinton?*

**Lösungen**

**1** Individual answers. Perot is the weakest candidate though, because he has no experience in politics at all. Clinton seems to have been the strongest in the debate, as the polls afterwards show.

**2** individual answers

**3** They react enthusiastically; Stephanopoulos repeatedly says that Bush was on the defensive. Clinton came in first in the polls. Bush 2nd and Perot 3rd. Clinton could win 2/3 of the TV audience, leading with 41% in the polls after the debate.

## 3. Post-viewing Activities

### Worksheet 35: Media and Politics – Your Opinion

**Didaktische Anmerkungen**

Dieses Arbeitsblatt bezieht sich auf alle drei Filme. Die SuS sollen abschließend zur medialen Darstellung von Politik Stellung nehmen und mögliche Gefahren durch eine zu große Medienpräsenz und Medienabhängigkeit diskutieren.

**Aufgaben**

**1** *To what extent has the film / have these films changed your attitude towards politics?*

**2** *Is the influence of the media dangerous for democratic elections?*

**Lösungen**

**1** Individual answers. The students should note though, that the viewer / voter should not believe everything politicians say and should not think that politicians are always the authors of their speeches and even thoughts. The voter has to be critical and careful about his decision. Politicians promise a lot and normally keep little, as Bud Johnsson mentions in his speech before the debate. The manipulation of the voter is certainly not as extensive as shown in Wag the Dog but certainly facts and numbers are spun to look better to the public.

**2** Individual answers. Due to legal regulations concerning democratic elections the influence of the media is limited if it comes to manipulation or even falsification. To distract the viewer from the main points of the election such as economy, social security and health issues might be a danger for the outcome of the election. If personal failures of a candidate are of more importance than his political skills, the voter is unable to decide without prejudice. Slinging mud is a danger for elections because the real issues are rendered unimportant, and mud-slinging is mainly done by the media, meaning that the media and not political views take center-stage.

# Worksheets

# American Politics: Basic Information

**1** *What do you know about the American electoral system?*

**2** *Who are these candidates? What do you know about them and what they stand / stood for?*

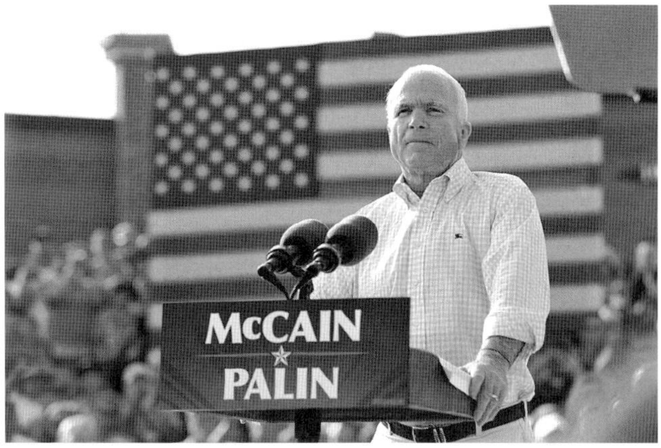

ISBN 978-3-12-577467-4

# Glossary of Political Terms (1)

**The Campaign**

| | |
|---|---|
| to build a machine | to assemble a campaign organisation of associates, supporters and consultants for support in the campaign race through the USA |
| candidate | a person who runs for an elected office |
| campaign | a series of political actions (like advertisements, public appearances, and debates) that are used to help a candidate get elected to office |
| caucus | a meeting of people who elect delegates and discuss issues for party platforms |
| delegate | a representative who supports the candidate's nomination at the national party convention |
| to fight it out | the candidate competes with his rivals from his own party in primaries and caucuses |
| to fill the treasury | to pay for the immense costs of a presidential campaign, the candidate contact individuals and groups, quite often big business companies |
| to hit the road | the candidates tour the nation looking for supporters and people to help them organise the campaign |
| the last spurt | the last months before the election, when the candidate tours the country holding speeches, taking part in debates, giving interviews and appearing on TV |
| money raiser | here: sb who collects money for a candidate or political party |
| to nominate | to choose and vote for a candidate |
| nominee | The person that a political party chooses to represent it in a general election. Nominees may be selected in primary elections or caucuses. When only one candidate from a party has filed to run for a political office, that candidate becomes the party's nominee without any further selection process |
| party platform | here: a political party's formal written statement of its principles and goals, put together and issued during the presidential nomination process and subject to approval affirmed during the party's national political convention. |
| poll | a place where votes are cast ; also refers to a survey to assess public opinion or to forecast an election. |
| primary election | an election in which voters choose the party candidates who will run for office |
| open primary / closed primary | election in which any registered voter in a state can vote for a candidate / election in which only registered voters who belong to a particular political party can vote for a candidate |
| to promote | to advertise |
| running mate | the person chosen to run with someone to help him/her win an election |
| to seize the banner | the party delegates nominate their presidential candidates at national conventions |
| to test the waters | the candidate tries to find out his chances of making the presidential race |
| swing states | A state in which no candidate has overwhelming support, meaning that any of the major candidates have a reasonable chance of winning the state's electoral college votes. Such states are targets of both major political parties in presidential elections, since winning these states is the best opportunity for a party to gain votes. Non-swing states are sometimes called safe states, because one candidate has strong enough support that they can safely assume they will win the state's votes. |
| | |
| | |
| | |
| | |


ISBN 978-3-12-577467-4

# Glossary of Political Terms (2)

## The Election

| | |
|---|---|
| ballot | a piece of paper listing the candidates running for office. A ballot is used to cast a vote. |
| to cast a vote | to register a vote |
| electoral college | the group of people that elects the president and vice president after the general election in the USA |
| electoral votes | the number of votes each state has (based on the number of people who live in that state) |
| to gain | to get, to achieve |
| majority | more than half of the votes |
| popular vote | the result based solely on the number of votes from qualified voters. The winner of the popular vote usually wins the election. |
| electors | anyone who can vote. In the US you have to register to vote, otherwise you can't vote. |
| presidential election debate | The main candidates of the two main parties, engage in a debate. The topics discussed in the debate are often the most controversial issues of the time.<br>Presidential debates are held late in the election cycle, after the political parties have nominated their candidates. The formats of the debates have varied, with questions sometimes posed from one or more journalist moderators and in other cases members of the audience.<br>Debates are broadcast live on television and radio. |
| direct election | the voters directly cast ballots for the person, persons or political party that they desire to see elected |
| indirect election | Voters in an election do not actually choose between candidates for an office but rather elect persons who will then make the choice.<br>Voters elect a slate of candidates for the Electoral College, which in turn elects the President. |
| | |
| | |
| | |
| | |

## After the Election

| | |
|---|---|
| inaugural address | speech given at the beginning of a political administration |
| oath | a sworn promise |
| office | here: an official position in government |
| presidency | the time period a president is elected for |
| turnout | result of the election |
| | |
| | |
| | |
| | |




ISBN 978-3-12-577467-4

# Elephant and Donkey: The Political Parties

**Republican Party**

The Republican Party was founded in 1854 by anti-slavery expansion activists. There are many famous Republican presidents: Abraham Lincoln, Theodore Roosevelt and Ronald Reagan. George W. Bush was the 19th Republican to hold office. The Republicans are supported by business because they favor a free-market and business and economic liberalism. They favor private spending rather than government spending and apply this attitude to the welfare system too, in the form of government grants for organizations to minimize abuse. Republicans believe that strict environmental standards hurt businesses. The Republican Party has always advocated a strong national defense and supports unilateralism in issues of national security, and the ability and right of the United States to act without external or international support in its own self-interest. Only the best-trained and best-equipped army can guarantee safety. Republican voters are white, Protestant, married with children and only a minority of them has a college degree. Young voters, single-parents and homosexuals are not core Republican voters. Since 1980, geographically the Republican «base» is strongest in the South and West, and dominate rural areas and suburbs.

**Democratic Party**

The Democratic Party was founded in 1792. Harry Truman, John F. Kennedy and Bill Clinton were all Democratic presidents. Democrats generally call for higher taxes on the rich and reduced taxes on the poor and middle classes, and reduced government spending to keep national debt and the budget deficit under control. Democrats are against cuts in education and social programs, arguing their place in American society to assist the disadvantaged and the poor. The welfare system should be supported by the government to guarantee care for everyone. Since the 1970s, environmental issues have played a major role in policies. Democrats have opposed tax cuts and incentives to oil companies. Democrats usually oppose unilateralism. They believe the United States should act in the international arena within strong alliances and international support, reducing the money spent on the military. The Democrats are traditionally supported by African-Americans, Jews, Catholics, Labor Unions, Liberals, the disadvantaged and the poor. It has many well-educated young voters. It is now strongest in the Northeast, Great Lakes region, and along the Pacific Coast. The Democrats are also strongest in major cities.

**1** *List the main differences between the two parties.*

**2** *Find corresponding parties in Germany and compare the parties' programs.*

**3** *Choose an issue from the excerpt you are interested in and find out more details on the parties' websites or the summary of issues on* http://edition.cnn.com/ELECTION/2008/issues/index.html

2 **anti-slavery expansion activists**: movement that was against slavery – 9 **spending** *here:* investing – 11 **grant** (noun): money given for a particular purpose – 15 **to advocate** to publicly recommend or support – 16 **unilateralism** the process of acting, reaching a decision, or supporting a principle without the agreement of others – 43 **to oppose**: to disapprove of and attempt to prevent – 44 **incentive**: a thing that motivates or encourages one to do something; here: benefits for the companies such as tax cuts – 47 **alliance**: an association to further the common interests of its members


ISBN 978-3-12-577467-4

# How to Become President

**1** The candidates are chosen: The presidential candidate has to be a native-born citizen of the United States, at least 35 years of age and have been a resident of the U.S. for at least 14 years. He can only be re-elected ONCE for another term of 4 years. (You can vote for the president if you are at least 18 years old and have registered to vote in your hometown.)
The first stage of a presidential campaign is the nomination campaign. Several candidates within the same party are competing against each other, each of them hoping to get the party's nomination. A majority of delegate votes is needed to win the party's nomination. In most cases, the delegates let their chosen presidential candidate select a vice-presidential candidate, their "running mate".

⇩

**2** Caucuses and Primary Elections take place: Caucuses and primaries give the general public the opportunity to take part in the nomination of presidential candidates. They take place from January to July in the election year. A caucus is a meeting at the local level in which registered members of a political party meet to express support for a candidate. Primaries are state-level elections in which voters choose a candidate [1]affiliated with a political party to run against a candidate who is affiliated with another political party in a later, general election. A primary may be either open or closed.

⇩

**3** The National Conventions: The main reason for holding national party conventions is to unify party members behind the party's platform and nominees. After the presidential candidates of each party have been selected at these conventions, the process of the general election begins. The candidates campaign through the USA to promote their ideas, gain publicity and popular votes. The conventions take place from July to September in the election year.

⇩

**4** Election Day: The campaign ends on Election Day, traditionally the Tuesday after the first Monday in November. Voters now cast their ballots to vote for the president and vice President. They don't vote for the President directly but indirectly through the Electoral College. The presidential election consists of 51 separate elections (number of states of US) where the voters are really voting for "electors" who then vote for the president.

⇩

**5** The Electoral College: The Electoral College votes for president and vice president, each elector casting one electoral vote. Normally, one of the candidates for president receives a majority of the electoral votes; that person is elected president. That candidate's vice
presidential running mate will then also receive a majority of electoral votes. Just before Christmas in the election year, [2]federal and state officials must have the electoral votes in Washington, DC, to confirm the candidate's election by counting the electoral votes for a last time.

⇩

**6** The President moves into the White House: on January 20, the president enters office by taking the presidential oath at a formal ceremony, the inauguration.

*Compare this to the electoral system in Germany and discuss the advantages and disadvantages of each system.*

1 **to be affiliated with** to be connected to, to belong to
2 **federal** of or describing a union of states with a central government;referring to that government



ISBN 978-3-12-577467-4

# An Election Quiz

*Fill in the blanks.*

**1** Every ______________ years the people of the United States vote for a new President.

**2** You have to be at least ______________ years old to run for President.

**3** There were two candidates from the same party in 2008. What were their names?

____________________________ ____________________________

**4** Who was the candidate for the other party? ____________________________

**5** In order to present themselves to the voters the candidates travel through the country, another expression for this is to ____________________________

**6** Candidates try to get people to vote for them by giving ____________________________ and shaking ____________________________.

**7** The political parties choose their candidate at their ____________________________.

**8** The candidates have ____________________________ where they answer questions about the issues that are important to the people in our country.

**9** On the Tuesday after the first Monday in ____________________________ people go to the polls to vote.

**10** People are particularly interested in the results from the states which tend to vote differently from one election to the next, or the ____________________________ states

**11** On ____________________________ the new president is sworn in, in Washington, D.C. in the ____________________________ ceremony.

**12** The President and his family move into the ____________________________ at 1600 Pennsylvania Avenue in Washington, D.C.


ISBN 978-3-12-577467-4

# The Manipulative Media: Analysis of Photos (1)

Photos can give you just as much information as texts – not "normal" written information, of course, but visual information, which can also be analysed. Of course, the analysis of pictures is different from the "normal" text analysis, but not more difficult! Worksheet 6 will help you not only to analyse photos, but also to become a critical viewer. You will learn to recognise when images try to manipulate their viewers, and also to find out the true meaning behind the pictures and to identify the visual elements for communicating a message.

*When you are about to analyse a photo, make sure you can answer the following questions as far as possible. Sometimes there is a caption beneath the picture, which will give you some information to start with.*

**1. First impression**

*What does the photo show, roughly? • Where and when was it taken? • Why was it taken? • What was your first reaction when looking at the photo? • What did you feel?*

______________________________

______________________________

______________________________

______________________________

______________________________

**Useful phrases**
The photo shows… • My first thought when seeing the picture was… • The photo reminds me of…/ … makes me think of…

**2. Description**

a) *Describe the photo. Start with the most important elements (those which caught your eye first) and then move to less striking aspects in the background or on the margin of the photo.*

______________________________

______________________________

______________________________

b) *Details may be important, too: the facial expression, body language, lighting, contrast of light and shadow and choice of colours, what is in focus and what in the background. What are the important details in this photo?*

______________________________

______________________________

______________________________

**Useful phrases**
In the middle/ centre there is/ there are… • At the top/ bottom…, • On the left/ right… • There is a contrast between the colours…./ … light and dark… • The… is in focus, but…. is out of focus/ blurry/blurred




ISBN 978-3-12-577467-4

# The Manipulative Media: Analysis of Photos (2)

### 3. Interpretation

*a) Describe the effect the photo has on you. What might the photo's message be?*

*b) Were photographic techniques such as close-up, medium shot or long shot used to transport the message?*

**Useful phrases**
**close-up** very near to an object or person, often showing just the face of a person • **medium shot** the person(s) are shown at least from the waist up • **long shot** complete objects and persons are shown together with their surroundings

### 4. Evaluation

*Now state what you think of the photo after carefully looking at and interpreting its elements. You should answer the following questions:*

*a) Does the picture succeed in bringing across the message to the intended group of people?*

*b) Which elements work particularly well, which could be changed or improved?*

**Useful phrases**
In my opinion, the picture is confusing/ authentic/ simplistic/ too complicated/ original/ nothing new... • My initial reaction to the picture was..., but on the second glance I think that.... • As can be seen from..., the picture's aim is to..., which it does very effectively/ skilfully/ convincingly... • Although the photographer manages to ..., the picture does/ does not reach the intended target group. • The point/ the message is driven home by...

*Analyse a photo of one of the presidential candidates / presidents of your choice following the method above.*


ISBN 978-3-12-577467-4

# Overview of Film Terminology (1)

## Camera Terms

ISBN 978-3-12-577467-4

# Overview of Film Terminology (2)

### Glossary of Film Terms 1

A shot is an uninterrupted piece of film from one point of view.
Shots may be categorized according to:
- the position and angle of the camera in relation to the object (see table I below);
- the distance between the camera and the object being filmed (see table II below).

### I: Position and angle of the camera (see p. 74)

| type of shot | camera position / angle | function |
|---|---|---|
| establishing shot | camera is placed at eyelevel and shows a particular scene | sets the scene for the action to come |
| eyelevel shot | camera is pointed at subject's eye level | gives the impression of authenticity and directness |
| high-angle shot | camera is positioned above the subject or object being filmed | makes a character seem vulnerable |
| low-angle shot | camera is positioned below a subject or object | enlarges sth and stresses its power / importance |
| overhead shot | gives an aerial view (bird's-eye view) e.g. of a town or an area | sets the scene; viewers are given an overall impression of the setting |
| over-the-shoulder shot | camera is placed behind one speaker and is pointed at a second speaker | viewers are given the impression that they are involved in the dialogue |
| reverse-angle shot | camera is placed behind the second speaker and focuses on the first dialogue partner | often used with the over-the-shoulder shot to give viewers both sides of a dialogue |

### II: Distance between the camera and the object (see p. 74)

| field size | technique | function |
|---|---|---|
| close-up | camera is very close to subject | concentrate viewers' attention on sth / sb specific; reveals feelings by showing sb's facial expressions |
| detail shot / extreme close up | camera is extremely close to a subject / object | gives particular attention to sth to show its importance in a scene |
| long shot | camera is at a great distance from the subject or object being filmed | presents an entire setting |
| medium shot | shows sb from the knees upwards | brings viewers closer to the the action |
| medium long shot / full shot | shows all of the subject and immediate surroundings | gives us a complete picture of sb or sth |


ISBN 978-3-12-577467-4

# Overview of Film Terminology (3)

### Glossary of Film Terms 2

### III: Camera movement

| camera movement | technique | function |
|---|---|---|
| hand-held camera | a way of moving the camera which seems to follow the rhythm of the person who is moving; pictures are often unclear | makes a situation seem more authentic |
| to pan left / right | the camera moves from left to right or right to left along a horizontal plane | e.g. follows a particular action; moves viewers attention from one thing to another |
| to tilt up / down | the camera moves up or down along a vertical plane | e.g. shows the subject in his / her full length |
| tracking shot | the camera is on a vehicle which is moving along the ground | allows viewers to follow a character's actions closely; adds speed to a scene |
| to zoom in / out | the camera moves quickly towards / away from the subject or object | concentrates attention on or moves attention away from sb or sth |

**IV: Transitions** (how shots are linked)

| types of transitions | technique | function |
|---|---|---|
| cut | switch from one image to the next; on the screen the appearance of the second shot immediately replaces the first | fast cuts give the impression of fast-paced action; slow cuts focus the viewer's attention, or create a calm atmosphere |
| to dissolve / mix | the end of one shot fades away and the second shot gradually becomes clearer | slow move from one scene to the next; it produces a special link or contrast between the two scenes |
| fade-in | a shot that begins in darkness and gradually becomes brighter | begins a scene slowly |
| fade-out | a shot that has an image at the beginning and gradually becomes darker until the screen is completely black | ends a scene in a memorable way |
| montage | refers to the assembly or editing of shots (see table V) | creates a meaningful relationship between the shots |
| sequence | an arrangement of shots | forms a coherent unit in the development of the plot |

**V: Types of montage** (editing or assembly of shots)

| types of montage | technique | function |
|---|---|---|
| cross-cut editing | technique of cutting back and forward between two scenes | shows that two things are happening simultaneously |
| flashback | a scene that breaks the chronological order of the plot by showing events which happened in the past | explains the origin of a problem and how it affects the present |
| flashforward | a scene that breaks the chronological order of the plot by showing events which happen or may happen in the future | gives an indication of events to come |
| freeze frame | an optical effect where one image is repeated | viewers have the impression that the action has stopped |
| parallel action | intermixing shots of two or more scenes | e.g. slows down / speeds up the action; gives extra information about the plot |




ISBN 978-3-12-577467-4

# Analysis of Campaign Ads (Videos)

*Choose a candidate and then choose a campaign video and watch it in your group. Take notes about the following aspects:*

1 *How is this ad divided into scenes? What are the dividing lines between scenes?*

2 *Is the ad too long? Too short? How important is the ad's length to delivering its message?*

3 *How does each scene relate to, or fit into, the ad's overall goal?*

4 *In your opinion, which scene(s) is the strongest? Why?*

*Now try to categorize the ad. Use specific examples from one or more candidates' ads to answer the following questions.*

5 *How would you categorize the ad (biographical, issue-oriented, value-laden, or negative)?*

6 *Describe the language and tone of the ad. Is the narrator male or female? Is the narrator the candidate? Does the ad specify an action for the viewer (i.e. to elect the candidate, to visit the candidate's website, to vote against the opponent)? How do language and tone shape the overall message?*

7 *How do words, images, colour, music, camera angles, lighting, people, and symbols contribute to the message of the ad? Do you think they are effective?*

8 *What is the goal of the ad? What is the candidate trying to achieve with his message? How does the ad attract the audience? Which voters is it intended to reach (retired / new / working / swing voters)?*

9 *What similarities, if any, can you find in each candidate's video? How do they contrast to one another? Put your findings into a table that can be photocopied (please type!)*


ISBN 978-3-12-577467-4

# The Presidential Debates: Structure of a Debate

*You are about to prepare a role play staging a Presidential Debate. You will choose a candidate and prepare his or her character with the help of worksheets and role cards. First, read the rules for a debate:*

The first Presidential Debate of the Campaign takes place on one of the major national TV stations at prime time. Millions of voters watch and make their decision about who they are going to vote for on November 4th. This is the chance for every candidate to leave a strong impression and gain electoral votes. There are rules for each debate that have to be agreed on in advance.

- Apart from a handshake at the beginning, the candidates are not to approach each other.
- No props, notes, charts, diagrams can be used by the candidates; however, they can take notes
- The candidates cannot address each other with proposed pledges
- The Coin Toss: There will be a coin toss about the order of questioning and closing arguments. The winner gets to choose whether to take the first or second question, or to make the first or second closing statement.
- A candidate gets two minutes to respond to a question: the other candidate gets 1½ minutes to comment on the question or to respond to his rival's answer. Each candidate gets two minutes for his opening and closing statement.
- The debate is led by a single moderator, who opens and closes the debate and enforces all time limits. Should the candidate exceed the permitted time for comment, the moderator will interrupt and remind both the candidate and the audience of that time has run out.
- The moderator should vary the topics on which the candidates are questioned and ensure that the topics of the questions are fairly distributed between the candidates, and also ensure that the candidates speak for more or less equal amounts of time during each debate.

**Useful phrases for a debate:**

| **Beginning a speech.** | **Listing arguments** | **Expressing disagreement** |
|---|---|---|
| • I saw/ read<br>• Have you ever thought about...?<br>• Did you know that...?<br>• What I would like to say is... | • First.... second... third<br>• In the first (second) place, ...<br>• Next, then furthermore, moreover<br>• Finally, last of all, to conclude | • That simply isn't true.<br>• It's not as simple as that.<br>• Are you sure?<br>• You're quite wrong there. |
| **Giving an opinion**<br>• In my opinion (view)...<br>• To my mind...<br>• As I see it...<br>If you ask me... | **Contrasting**<br>• On the contrary,...<br>• On the one hand... on the other hand | **Showing results**<br>• Therefore,...<br>• Consequently,...<br>• As a result,...<br>**Concluding**<br>• To sum up,...<br>• In conclusion... |

**10 Golden Rules for Debating**

1. Avoid the use of *never* and *always*; use of *generally* allows for exceptions.
2. Use *many* rather than *most* to avoid exaggeration.
3. Refrain from saying you are wrong, you can say your idea is mistake. Attack the idea not the person.
4. Don't disagree with obvious truths.
5. Quote sources and numbers.
6. If it is just an opinion, admit it and do not present opinion as facts.
7. Stress the positive, and concede minor or trivial points.
8. Avoid bickering, quarrelling, and wrangling..
9. Watch your tone of voice, and smile when disagreeing.
10. Don't win a debate and lose a friend. Keep your perspective – you're just debating.

5 **to approach** to come close to each other; 6 **props** objects used in a theatre performance; 6 **chart** table, graph; 7 **to propose** to plan; 7 **pledge** promise, vow; 10 **to respond** to answer; 13 **to enforce** to put in force; 14 **to exceed**: to go over; 14 **to be permitted**: to be allowed; 16 **to vary**: to differ



ISBN 978-3-12-577467-4

# The Presidential Debates: Roleplay Cards (1)

*Imagine you are a candidate for president or the moderator at the debates.*

*Prepare and carry out a debate.*

**Mrs. Haley Caldwell (Democrat), Senator of New Jersey**

You are a politically ambitious woman in your 50s. After a successful career as a lawyer you took a rest from your job because your husband became the president of the USA. After eight years full of political and private scandals you decided to turn your back on the law business and become a politician yourself.
Your campaign is not going well. You don't seem to be able to win enough delegates to win the nomination against Mr. Sanchez, a Democrat also running for office. Your campaign speeches become more and more aggressive because you definitely want to be nominated by your party as presidential candidate.
Your most important political stances are families and children. You want to improve the welfare system and the educational possibilities for the poor. As the First Lady you have been chairwoman of several welfare organisations concerning this topic and you want to expand this work as president.

**Howard W. Tree (Republican), Governor of Texas**

You are a married man in your 50s who comes from a politically and economically influential family. Your father has been a US president and various relatives hold influential political positions all over the US. You are used to getting what you want, and your family has enough money to support your campaign. You also have many friends in high places and are sure you'll win the presidency. With this arrogance you express your political stance. Like your father, you think that war against terrorism is important and that the president should be able to act freely and on his own in the case of decisions concerning foreign policy. You also think that foreign policy should enable the USA to attack other countries first in order to prevent them from endangering the USA. Additionally you think that the defence budget should be given $ 1 billion to finance the war in Afghanistan and Iraq. You don't want to waste money on welfare projects – private organisations can take care of that.

**Rodrigo Sanchez (Democrat), Major of Santa Fe, New Mexico**

Equal rights for all Americans are the major aim of your political stance. Being the son of Mexican immigrants you have worked hard to become a politically successful man. You present yourself as a man from the poor suburbs. You not only want to get the votes from the Hispanic community but see the potential power of this social stratum, being almost as big as the part of the African Americans in some states of the USA. You are a shining example of the American "From rags to riches". dream You were a good student at High School and won a scholarship to a good university where you studied foreign affairs and journalism. You have travelled to Afghanistan and Iraq as a journalist and are of the opinion that foreign troops are worsening the situation in these countries instead of improving it. You want to cut the defence budget and return the troops to the US. You would rather spend the money saved on education and support of disadvantaged youth. You don't want to rely on welfare organisations because you think these people should learn how to help themselves.


ISBN 978-3-12-577467-4

# The Presidential Debates: Roleplay Cards (2)

**Martha Power (Republican), Head of Power Corporation, USA's biggest food producing company**

You are a very successful business woman. You lead the family company and are one of the richest women in the world. You think that your success in business qualifies you for the job as US president. Your goal is to increase the influence of businesses and companies in US politics, in order to cut down debt and to enable them to influence the judicial branch for the purpose of the economy. The modern democracy doesn't work without the financial help of big companies such as yours. Regarding your company's interest, you are of the opinion that the cultivation of genetically engineered food must not only be legal, but must be a precondition for modern and effective farming. You want to enlarge the science budget to further the research of GE and thus to become the leading nation in the field of food production. The USA is a country with an unimaginable number of acres of farm land and you want to make this economic section the major one. You don't see any necessity in conserving nature as it is but think that nature has to be used for economic purposes.

**Moderator**

As the moderator of the first presidential debate you begin by introducing the participants briefly. You pose the questions for debate, and call the debate to order if necessary. After you have established who will begin (by tossing a coin), start off with the opening statements. Then ask the candidates the questions which you have prepared in your group. Keep in mind that the questions should be open enough to allow discussion; if the other candidates hesitate to make a statement, try to encourage them to do so. Remember to keep an eye on the time, stop a candidate if she or he exceeds the time limit. Include all of the candidates in the discussion; a debate is not a one man/ woman-show!




ISBN 978-3-12-577467-4

# The Speeches: Barack Obama, New Hampshire, Jan 8, 2008 (1)

I want to congratulate Senator Clinton on a hard-fought victory here in New Hampshire.

A few weeks ago, no one imagined that we'd have accomplished what we did here tonight. For most of this campaign, we were far behind, and we always knew our climb would be steep.

But in record numbers, you came out and spoke up for change. And with your voices and your votes, you made it clear that at this moment – in this election – there is something happening in America.

There is something happening when men and women in Des Moines and Davenport; in Lebanon and Concord come out in the snows of January to wait in lines that stretch block after block because they believe in what this country can be.

There is something happening when Americans who are young in age and in spirit – who have never before participated in politics – turn out in numbers we've never seen because they know in their hearts that this time must be different.

There is something happening when people vote not just for the party they belong to but the hopes they hold in common – that whether we are rich or poor; black or white; Latino or Asian; whether we hail from Iowa or New Hampshire, Nevada or South Carolina, we are ready to take this country in a fundamentally new direction. That is what's happening in America right now. Change is what's happening in America.

You can be the new majority who can lead this nation out of a long political darkness – Democrats, Independents and Republicans who are tired of the division and distraction that has clouded Washington; who know that we can disagree without being disagreeable; who understand that if we mobilize our voices to challenge the money and influence that's stood in our way and challenge ourselves to reach for something better, there's no problem we can't solve – no destiny we cannot fulfil.

Our new American majority can end the outrage of unaffordable, unavailable health care in our time. We can bring doctors and patients; workers and businesses, Democrats and Republicans together; and we can tell the drug and insurance industry that while they'll get a seat at the table, they don't get to buy every chair. Not this time. Not now.

Our new majority can end the tax breaks for corporations that ship our jobs overseas and put a middle-class tax cut into the pockets of the working Americans who deserve it.

We can stop sending our children to schools with corridors of shame and start putting them on a pathway to success. We can stop talking about how great teachers are and start rewarding them for their greatness. We can do this with our new majority.

We can harness the ingenuity of farmers and scientists; citizens and entrepreneurs to free this nation from the tyranny of oil and save our planet from a point of no return.

3 **steep** exorbitant, extraordinary; 7 **Des Moines, Davenport, Lebanon, Concord** names of cities in the USA, there are is only one Des Moines but several Davenports, Lebanons and Concords; 11 **to participate** to take an active part in; 15 **to hail** to call (over); 19 **distraction** diversion, disturbance; 21 **to challenge** to confront, to face up to; 24 **outrage** anger, fury; 24 **unaffordable** high-priced, too expensive; 28 **corporation** business, company; 33 **pathway** trail, corridor; 37 **to harness** to gather and use; 37 **ingenuity** cleverness, skill


ISBN 978-3-12-577467-4

# The Speeches: Barack Obama, New Hampshire, Jan 8, 2008 (2)

And when I am President, we will end this war in Iraq and bring our troops home; we will finish the job against al Qaeda in Afghanistan; we will care for our veterans; we will restore our moral standing in the world; and we will never use 9/11 as a way to scare up votes, because it is not a tactic to win an election, it is a challenge that should unite America and the world against the common threats of the twenty-first century: terrorism and nuclear weapons; climate change and poverty; genocide and disease.

All of the candidates in this race share these goals. All have good ideas. And all are patriots who serve this country honourably.

But the reason our campaign has always been different is because it's not just about what I will do as President, it's also about what you, the people who love this country, can do to change it.

That's why tonight belongs to you. It belongs to the organizers and the volunteers and the staff who believed in our improbable journey and rallied so many others to join.

We know the battle ahead will be long, but always remember that no matter what obstacles stand in our way, nothing can withstand the power of millions of voices calling for change.

We have been told we cannot do this by a chorus of cynics. They will only grow louder and more dissonant in the weeks to come. We've been asked to pause for a reality check. We've been warned against offering the people of this nation false hope.

But in the unlikely story that is America, there has never been anything false about hope. For when we have faced down impossible odds; when we've been told we're not ready, or that we shouldn't try, or that we can't, generations of Americans have responded with a simple creed that sums up the spirit of a people.

Yes we can. Yes we can. Yes we can.

It was a creed written into the founding documents that declared the destiny of a nation. Yes we can.

It was whispered by slaves and abolitionists as they blazed a trail toward freedom through the darkest of nights. Yes we can.

It was sung by immigrants as they struck out from distant shores and pioneers who pushed westward against an unforgiving wilderness. Yes we can.

It was the call of workers who organized; women who reached for the ballot; a President who chose the moon as our new frontier; and a King who took us to the mountaintop and pointed the way to the Promised Land.

Yes we can to justice and equality. Yes we can to opportunity and prosperity. Yes we can heal this nation. Yes we can repair this world. Yes we can.

And so tomorrow, as we take the campaign South and West; as we learn that the struggles of the textile worker in Spartanburg are not so different than the plight of the dishwasher in Las Vegas; that the hopes of the little girl who goes to a crumbling school in Dillon are the same as the dreams of the boy who learns on the streets of LA; we will remember that there is something happening in America; that we are not as divided as our politics suggests; that we are one people; we are one nation; and together, we will begin the next great chapter in the American story with three words that will ring from coast to coast; from sea to shining sea – Yes. We. Can.

Remarks of Senator Barack Obama on New Hampshire Primary Night, January 8th, 2008

2 **moral standing** ethical reputation; 3 **to scare up** to fright, to shock; 5 **genocide** the deliberate killing of a large group of people, especially those of a particular race or nation; 10 **volunteer** unpaid helper; 10 **staff** employees, personnel; 11 **improbable** *here :* impossible, unlikely to succeed; 12 **obstacle** barrier, problem; 13 **withstand** to resist; 14 **cynic** pessimist, doubter; 15 **dissonant** not harmonious, unmusical, sounding bad; 18 **to face down** to overcome sth by standing up to up; 18 **odds** chances, probability; 19 **creed** doctrine, belief; 22 **founding documents** Declaration of Independence (1776) and Bill of Rights; 22 **destiny** future, luck; 23 **abolitionist** a person who favours the end of slavery; 23 **to blaze** to burn; 27 **ballot** vote; 30 **prosperity** wealth, richness; 33 **plight** dilemma, troubles; 34 **to crumble** to fall apart, to fall to pieces




ISBN 978-3-12-577467-4

# The Speeches: Barack Obama, New Hampshire, Jan 8, 2008 (3)

**1** *What is the occasion and the purpose of this speech? Use the Internet to help you.*

**2** *Describe the structure of the speech.*

**3** *What stylistic and rhetorical devices does Obama use? Give examples.*

**4** *How effective do you think this speech was in the 2008 presidential campaign?*


ISBN 978-3-12-577467-4

## Interpretation of Film Poster and Title

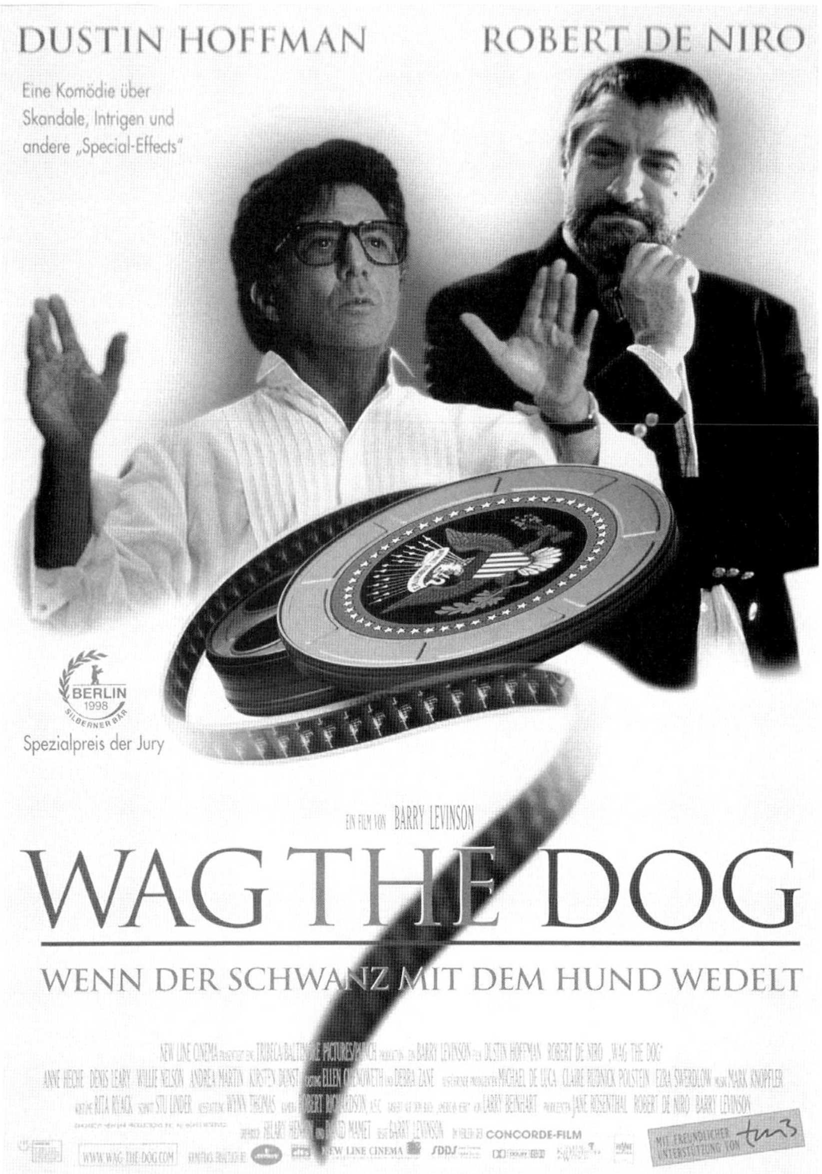


**1** *Jot down your first thoughts about the title and the poster of the movie.*

**2** *Write in ONE short sentence on your flashcard what you think the movie might be about and put your flashcard on the board.*




ISBN 978-3-12-577467-4

# The Trailer

**1** *Watch the trailer. Answer the following questions:*

**a)** *What is the plot of the movie about?*

**b)** *Where does it take place?*

**c)** *Who play the main characters?*

**2** *Write a short summary of the movie with just the information from the trailer as a basis.*


ISBN 978-3-12-577467-4

## A Political Scandal

*In* Wag the Dog *the political problem is the president's sexual assault of a student in the White House. There have been scandals about US presidents in the past. Get together in groups of four and research on ONE of the following political scandals. The websites are not the only source; they are only a hint to get you started. You should search for further information on other websites.*

1 **The Watergate affair**: http://www.washingtonpost.com/wp-srv/politics/special/watergate/#chapters
2 **The Lewinsky scandal**: http://edition.cnn.com/ALLPOLITICS/1998/resources/lewinsky/timeline/
3 **Presidential Election 2000**: http://election2000.stanford.edu/
4 **Rutherford B. Hayes' election 1876**: http://www.whitehouse.gov/about/presidents/RutherfordBHayes/
5 **The Chappaquiddick incident**: http://www.telegraph.co.uk/news/worldnews/northamerica/usa/6094161/Ted-Kennedy-Chappaquiddick-Incident.html

---


## A Political Scandal

*In* Wag the Dog *the political problem is the president's sexual assault of a student in the White House. There have been scandals about US presidents in the past. Get together in groups of four and research on ONE of the following political scandals. The websites are not the only source; they are only a hint to get you started. You should search for further information on other websites.*

1 **The Watergate affair**: http://www.washingtonpost.com/wp-srv/politics/special/watergate/#chapters
2 **The Lewinsky scandal**: http://edition.cnn.com/ALLPOLITICS/1998/resources/lewinsky/timeline/
3 **Presidential Election 2000**: http://election2000.stanford.edu/
4 **Rutherford B. Hayes' election 1876**: http://www.whitehouse.gov/about/presidents/RutherfordBHayes/
5 **The Chappaquiddick incident**: http://www.telegraph.co.uk/news/worldnews/northamerica/usa/6094161/Ted-Kennedy-Chappaquiddick-Incident.html


---


## A Political Scandal

*In* Wag the Dog *the political problem is the president's sexual assault of a student in the White House. There have been scandals about US presidents in the past. Get together in groups of four and research on ONE of the following political scandals. The websites are not the only source; they are only a hint to get you started. You should search for further information on other websites.*

1 **The Watergate affair**: http://www.washingtonpost.com/wp-srv/politics/special/watergate/#chapters
2 **The Lewinsky scandal**: http://edition.cnn.com/ALLPOLITICS/1998/resources/lewinsky/timeline/
3 **Presidential Election 2000**: http://election2000.stanford.edu/
4 **Rutherford B. Hayes' election 1876**: http://www.whitehouse.gov/about/presidents/RutherfordBHayes/
5 **The Chappaquiddick incident**: http://www.telegraph.co.uk/news/worldnews/northamerica/usa/6094161/Ted-Kennedy-Chappaquiddick-Incident.html





ISBN 978-3-12-577467-4

# Fishbowl Discussion:
# How Damaging are Political Scandals for a Nation's Leader?

Your teacher will ask you to write down in one sentence which effect(s) you think a political scandal might have on a nation's political leader.

*After you have collected everyone's thoughts you will have a fishbowl-discussion about the various aspects you have collected. For this special discussion method the following steps have to be taken:*

1 *Arrange a circle of chairs in the centre of the room with chairs arranged around the outside;*
2 *A few participants either volunteer or are selected to fill the fishbowl, while the rest of the group sits on the chairs outside the fishbowl;*
3 *One chair in the inner circle is left empty. The topic is introduced and the participants start discussing;*
4 *The audience outside the fishbowl listens in on the discussion. If an observer has a burning comment to contribute, he/she quickly moves to the hot seat to join the fishbowl, then exits once his/her comment has been voiced.*

---

# Fishbowl Discussion:
# How Damaging are Political Scandals for a Nation's Leader?

Your teacher will ask you to write down in one sentence which effect(s) you think a political scandal might have on a nation's political leader.

*After you have collected everyone's thoughts you will have a fishbowl-discussion about the various aspects you have collected. For this special discussion method the following steps have to be taken:*

1 *Arrange a circle of chairs in the centre of the room with chairs arranged around the outside;*
2 *A few participants either volunteer or are selected to fill the fishbowl, while the rest of the group sits on the chairs outside the fishbowl;*
3 *One chair in the inner circle is left empty. The topic is introduced and the participants start discussing;*
4 *The audience outside the fishbowl listens in on the discussion. If an observer has a burning comment to contribute, he/she quickly moves to the hot seat to join the fishbowl, then exits once his/her comment has been voiced.*

---

# Fishbowl Discussion:
# How Damaging are Political Scandals for a Nation's Leader?

Your teacher will ask you to write down in one sentence which effect(s) you think a political scandal might have on a nation's political leader.

*After you have collected everyone's thoughts you will have a fishbowl-discussion about the various aspects you have collected. For this special discussion method the following steps have to be taken:*

1 *Arrange a circle of chairs in the centre of the room with chairs arranged around the outside;*
2 *A few participants either volunteer or are selected to fill the fishbowl, while the rest of the group sits on the chairs outside the fishbowl;*
3 *One chair in the inner circle is left empty. The topic is introduced and the participants start discussing;*
4 *The audience outside the fishbowl listens in on the discussion. If an observer has a burning comment to contribute, he/she quickly moves to the hot seat to join the fishbowl, then exits once his/her comment has been voiced.*


ISBN 978-3-12-577467-4

# Characters and Characterization

Characters are people endowed with moral and dispositional qualities that are expressed in what they say and what they do. A character has character traits: he or she may be shy, self-confident, sensitive, ambitious, and so on. In movies these character traits are shown by a character's actions, language, thoughts and interaction with other characters. A character might remain stable (flat character) or he may undergo a change and develop in the course of a movie (round character).

Showing techniques ("indirect characterization") are almost the same as those used by a dramatist (appearance, actions, language, thoughts, interaction). The director of a movie presents the characters talking and acting a leaves the viewer to infer what motives and dispositions lie behind. With telling techniques ("direct characterisation") the director lets a narrator from the off inform the viewer directly about what characters are like.

**Aspects of characterization**

Begin with the exterior / "objective" information, the outward appearance

| | |
|---|---|
| sex | |
| age | |
| profession | |
| position in life | |

and then go into more detail :

**behaviour towards others**

**other's reactions to character**

**feelings and attitudes**

**words and thoughts**

*Describe the character of the president's staff in as much detail as possible*




ISBN 978-3-12-577467-4

# Scene Analysis: The Opening Scene

**1** *Watch the first scene of the movie (ch. 3, 1:25-3:05) and focus on the following aspects:*

| | |
|---|---|
| **a) action** | |
| → time and place of the action | |
| → atmosphere | |
| → events | |
| **b) characters** | |
| → description of characters | |
| → impression characters have on the viewer concerning outward appearance, body language and choice of words. | |
| **c) cinematic devices and their function (use Worksheet 7):** | |
| → camera operations (field sizes, movements, positions, angles) | |
| → symbols | |
| → music, sounds | |

**2** *Now that you've gathered information, interpret the scene, giving reasons why the director chose to open the movie with it.*

**3** *Give your personal opinion about the scene. Does it leave an impression? Does it make you want to keep watching?*


ISBN 978-3-12-577467-4

# The War Begins (1)

*Watch the scene from the movie where the war report is prepared.* (ch. 3 1:25-3:05)

A big, empty, blue room, film set, busy film crew members running around, Motss arrives with his assistant and meets the main character, a young woman in "Albanian" clothes.

**MOTSS :** Hi, my name's Stanley Motss, I'll be your producer this morning, what I'd like you to do, Miss, what is your name…?

**Young woman:** Tracy Lime.

**MOTSS:** "Tracy," stand against that wall… (*gestures into the distance*) and, on my signal, "action" running I want you toward me, screaming … Can I get you anything?

**TRACY:** Fine. (*Shakes her head)*

**MOTSS :** A cup of tea? A little milk, low fat? No? You're okay? Let's just try one, why don't we just try one.

**TRACY:** Is this a national? Is that the case? Because my agent didn't get a chance to…

**MOTSS:** Well, it's a little bit of a…

**Assistant:** …we're going for a direct buy-out.

**MOTSS:** …why don't you just have your agent check with the…

**TRACY:** No, I know it's going to be fine. I'm so excited, and I'm looking forward to putting it on my resume. When you called last…

(*while she speaks MOTSS walks over to the pet trainers complaining about the dogs because he wanted kittens, while Brean takes Tracy aside*)

**BREAN:** Eh, Tracy, could I talk to you for a minute please? This is a special kind of situation; it's a funny kind of situation

*AMES comes over to the pet trainers, holding a cellphone.*

**AMES:** (*describing the scene into his phone*) Well; we have a schnauzer. What appears to be a…

**PET TRAINER:** Lhasa Apso.

**AMES:** (into phone) Lhasa Apso, and a…

**MOTSS:** It couldn't have been simpler

*looks at the third dog*

**PET WRANGLER:** What you got here is a basically a cross between a dog and what is substantially a…

**MOTSS:** I don't want a cross, I just want a kitten.

*AMES gestures he should be quiet, listens to his phone.*

**AMES :** (*into the phone*) Abso… absolutely, sir… Absolutely. (*to MOTSS*) The president would like a kitten. (*walking away*) We'll get a kitten.

**MOTSS:** No, I want a kitten, away with all the dogs, just keep the kitten.

*AMES walks over to BREAN and TRACY.*

**AMES:** Miss, we are going to have to have you sign this little sheet of paper here …

**TRACY:** Well, my agent would be real real mad with me, if I signed anything, uh, to …

**AMES:** This has nothing to do with your deal. This is your (PAUSE) security clearance. Right there.

*TRACY signs.*

**AMES:** Nice signature, thank you, Tracy.

**BREAN:** Nice seeing you, Tracy.

**PET TRAINER:** This is a nice one.

**MOTSS:** But that's not a kitten, it's a cat, these are kittens.

**MOTSS' FEMALE ASSISTANT:** They just want to give you some options.

**MOTSS:** Yes, but it's too confusing. And that guy keeps pushing the Lapso Apso.

**2nd ASSISTANT (TO MOTSS):** …fix it in the mix. We'll do it optical.

**ASSISTANT:** We're going to do it digitally…

**MOTSS:** …can we shoot one? Ok, Stacy…




ISBN 978-3-12-577467-4

Klett

# The War Begins (2)

**TRACY:** Tracy.

**MOTSS:** Tracy. I want you to stand right over here, ok, here you go, right there …

*ASSISTANT hands TRACY a bag of potato chips.*

**TRACY:** … these are chips …

**2nd ASSISTANT:** Just hold the bag when you run.

**MOTSS**: (*to TRACY*) We need it for the arm position, on the screen it'll be a kitten.

**TRACY:** Can I hold the kitten …?

**MOTSS:** No, we'll punch it in later. Right there

**TRACY:** … you're gonna punch the kitten later?

**MOTSS:** Yes.

**TRACY:** Why …?

**ASSISTANT**: (*in the background*) Okay, settle, people. Settle… we're gonna try one…

**MOTSS:** For a wider set of options.

**TRACY:** A wider option of what?

**MOTSS:** (*distracted*) Of kittens.

*TRACY adresses BREAN.*

**TRACY:** Sir, all kidding aside. When this goes national, I get to put it on my resume?

**BREAN:** Actually, no.

**TRACY:** Because, like, what is it, a guild thing or something? I mean, …

**BREAN:** You can never tell anyone you did this.

**TRACY:** … what, what could they do to me …

**BREAN:** (*smiling*): They'd come home to your house and kill you. (*gets handed a phone with the words: "The president."*)

**ASSISTANT:** (*to Hair and Make-up*): Stop the make up. She's just been raped by Terrorists, jump out, please.

**BREAN:** (*into phone*): They're starting to shoot now and they'll do the kitten thing optically. Yes, that's right, Mr. President. I don't know how they'll do the kitten optically, but..

*BREAN wanders off, still talking into his phone.*

**AMES:** Sir, she's not an illegal immigrant, Is she? Could I see the contract, please? Because the president cannot employ an illegal immigrant. Let me see.

**MOTSS:** (*getting a hair-do by the stylist, screaming in the direction of the crew*) Just use more spray. Let's keep working, people. Are we getting there?

*Transcript from* "Wag the Dog"

**1** *Describe the atmosphere on set. Pay special attention to the relationship between Ames, Brean and Motss.*


ISBN 978-3-12-577467-4

# The War Begins (3)

**2** *The stage is set for shooting the actual newscast. Get together in groups and continue the screenplay individually actually "shooting" the report for the national evening news on US television.*
*– Remember, the report has to get the viewer's attention and persuade him that there really is a war between the US and Albania, so think of catchy special effects or props. The report will be shot in front of a blue screen, where anything can be "punched in" digitally, so use your options!*
*Think of what war reports look like on TV and include as much aspects you know as possible:*
*Your news report shouldn't be any longer than 2 minutes.*
*– When you've finished with writing your screenplay, practise the report, you will perform it in front of the class.*

**3** *Now watch the report Stanley Motss produced. How does this report underline Motss' ingenuity as a producer?*



ISBN 978-3-12-577467-4

# After the End of the War

**1** *Watch the movie until* ch. 11, 45:40.

Senator Neall has ended the war and wants the president to comment on the new situation. Brean and Ames are devastated; there are only 7 days to Election Day.

**2** *First, speculate about how the movie will continue and take notes on a flash card.*

**3** *Imagine the following situation: YOU are Stanley Motss. When Brean and Ames desperately ask you for help in this hopeless situation you instantly have an idea what to do, the campaign will not be stopped but merely changed. There still is hope for the re-election of the president, because "This is nothing!":*

a) *Your new campaign strategy will be:*

b) *and this will be put into action as follows:*


ISBN 978-3-12-577467-4

# Analysis of Campaign Ads: Never Change Horses in Midstream

*There are four different campaign ads for the re-election of the president. Get together in groups and analyse ONE of the ads in the following manner:*

**1** *Analyse the use of cinematic devices in the following manner:*

*a) Which field sizes were used?*

---

*b) Which camera movements were used?*

---

*c) Which camera positions were used?*

---

*d) Which camera angles were used?*

---

*e) How are shots linked or edited*

---

*f) How is music used?*

---

**2** *Now that you've got the film techniques, analyse in what way they cause an effect on the viewer to re-elect the president.*

---

---

---

---

**3** *Give your personal opinion about the campaign ad you have worked with.*

---

---

---

---




ISBN 978-3-12-577467-4

# Scene Analysis: The Burial of a War Hero (1)

**1** *Listen closely to the song and try to understand as much of the text as possible. What is your first impression? Do you like the song?*

**2** *What is the song about? Is it a special kind of song?*

**3** *Now read the lyrics of the song and analyse it in more detail.*

**God Bless the Men of the 303**

We're gathered here,
With a cross to bear
The bravest men
Anywhere,
That this great land
Will remain free,
God bless the men
Of the 303

Side by side
We know no fear,
Our minds are sharp,
Our eyes are clear.
In the air, on land
Or on the sea,
We're the fighting men
Of the 303.

303
Give us this day
Our daily bread,
And leopard skin
For our head,
That we may fight …

© Written by Huey Lewis, performed by Scott Matthews, Johnny Colla and Huey Lewis. *Wag The Dog* 1997


ISBN 978-3-12-577467-4

# Scene Analysis: The Burial of a War Hero (2)

**4** *Now that you know the lyrics, has your impression of the song changed?*

**5** Watch *the burial of William Schumann (ch. 18, 01:21:20 – 01:22:30) at which the song of the "303" can be heard. Now that you've already analysed the song, pay close attention to the pictures, namely*

*a) the course of the funeral service*

*b) the soldiers' clothes*

**6** *Comment on the song as background music for William Schumann's funeral.*




ISBN 978-3-12-577467-4

# Politicians: Powerful Leaders or Puppets of the Media?

*Now that you've watched the complete movie, focus on the politicians Senator Neal and the president.*

**1** *Describe Senator Neal's and the President's character in keywords only with aspects you remember from the movie.*

| Senator Neal | The President |
|---|---|
| | |

**2** *Which one of them seems to be more able to be the leader of a nation as powerful and influential as the USA?*

**3** *Analyse the President's speech in* ch.13, 56:30.

**a)** *Analyse the structure of the speech and find stylistic devices that support the appealing character of the speech.*

**b)** *Elaborate on why the speech was so touching and thus helpful for the president's re-election.*


ISBN 978-3-12-577467-4

# Writing a Review

### Preparation
In order to write a review, you will have to decide which opinion(s) you wish to present. Collect material – arguments and examples – to support what you want to say. Now organise the material you have gathered. Focus on the stronger points – you can leave out the very weak ones – you don't have to cover every aspect of a film in a review (although it often sounds more balanced if you do). It's usually a good idea to begin with your weaker points so that you can end with the stronger ones.

### Title
Choose the title of the movie. Puns and allusion are allowed, too; they can be quite entertaining.

### Introduction
Start off with information about the film. If the movie has won an award, you could mention it in this part of the text. Is the director or are the actors famous or even academy award winners? Are they known for a certain genre? Is the movie a remake, a documentary or a sequel?

### Main part
Give a brief summary of the plot, without referring to specific scenes. Always remember that you are writing for readers who don't know the movie yet! Your task as a reviewer is to give an opinion of the movie. But don't only write "I didn't like this fantasy movie", but aim for more information : "The computer-animated scenes were good, but lacked technical knowledge to be truly convincing." Give reasons for your opinion.
Grab the readers attention in the first or «lead» paragraph in one of several ways: Start with a quote from the movie, and explain how it reflects the movie; refer to the reputation of the actor or director and compare it to how he or she did in this movie; compare this movie to another well-known film in a sentence or two; explain what your expectation was, and then if it was fulfilled or not. But: don't give too many details about the movie, remember, the reader might want to see it after having read your review. Introduce the main characters. How did you like their performance? Did you identify with a certain character? Were the actors believable and likeable? Then end the first paragraph by writing your opinion statement.
Be interesting and brief. Some readers might read the review just before going to the movies and need the information quickly!

### Conclusion
Either recommend the film, advise against seeing it, or give it a rating (for example, three stars out of five). Make sure that your final judgement is logically developed from what you have written before.

*Write a review about the movie, making clear why you think it is a good or bad movie.*



ISBN 978-3-12-577467-4

# Interpretation of Film Poster and Title

**1** *Jot down your first thoughts about the title and the poster of the movie.*

______________________________________________________________________

______________________________________________________________________

______________________________________________________________________

**2** *Write in ONE short sentence on your flashcard what you think the movie might be about and put your flashcard on the board.*

______________________________________________________________________

______________________________________________________________________


ISBN 978-3-12-577467-4

# The Trailer

**1** *Watch the trailer. Answer the following questions:*

**a)** *What is the plot of the movie about?*

**b)** *Where does it take place?*

**c)** *Who play the main characters?*

**2** *Write a short summary of the movie with just the information from the trailer as a basis.*




ISBN 978-3-12-577467-4

# Characters and Characterisation

**1** Watch the first two chapters of the movie and characterise Bud and Molly.

| | **Bud** | **Molly** |
|---|---|---|
| outward appearance | | |
| behaviour, words and thoughts | | |
| others' reactions | | |
| feelings and attitudes | | |

**2** *Describe Molly's and Bud's attitudes to politics.*

**3** *What do you think about voting? Give reasons for your opinion.*


ISBN 978-3-12-577467-4

# A Letter to Bud

*Watch the movie up to chapter 5. Imagine you were one of the candidates and had the opportunity to write one letter to Bud to convince him to vote for you. Write the letter.*




ISBN 978-3-12-577467-4

# The Campaign Managers

**1** *Describe the characters of the president's and Greenleaf's campaign managers.*

| The President's Manager: Martin Fox | Greenleaf's Manager, Art Crumb |
|---|---|
| | |

**2** *"The campaign managers in* Swing Vote *bear a resemblance to Conrad Brean from* Wag the Dog.*" Comment on this statement.*


ISBN 978-3-12-577467-4

# Bud's Speech

**1** *Taking into consideration what you have found out about Barack Obama's promises in the campaign 2008, which questions would you think are of major interest in a debate and could influence a swing voter's decision? Write them on a flash card and put them on the board.*

**2** *Analyse Bud's speech before the debate, ch.10 (1:44) paying special attention to the use of stylistic devices.*

**3** *Comment on the speech.*




ISBN 978-3-12-577467-4

# Radio Interview

**1** *What is the purpose of the interview?*

**2** *What's the atmosphere between Costner and the radio show host like?*

**3** *How does Costner handle the host's criticism concerning the movie?*

**4** *Comment on the host's statement: "Now I have to say, though, that as we're talking about both sides being represented as being pretty flimsy, in the end, it does seem like the correct stand on the issues in this movie is pretty left of center".*


ISBN 978-3-12-577467-4

# A Political Documentary

1 *Imagine a presidential candidate asked you to make a documentary about his or her campaign. What would be the most important events you'd include in the documentary? Write your ideas on a flashcard.*

2 *What would be the differences to a movie like* Wag the Dog *or* Swing Vote*? Would the movies have anything in common? Take notes.*

3 *Watch the trailer (twice) on http://www.imdb.com/video/screenplay/vi1140588825/ and pay special attention on both events and film techniques. Take notes.*




ISBN 978-3-12-577467-4

# A Real Campaign

**1** *Take notes about the different stages of a real campaign.*

**2** *What are the main problems for the campaign managers and how do they solve them?*

**3** *What is the relationship between the candidate and the campaign manager like? Can you compare it to the relationship as shown in either* Wag the Dog *or* Swing Vote*?*


ISBN 978-3-12-577467-4

# Stephanopoulos und Carville

*Analyse either Stephanopoulos conversation on the telephone with an unknown person or Carville's speech to the campaign team on election night, paying particular attention to the men's skills as campaign managers.*




ISBN 978-3-12-577467-4

# The Debate

*Watch the 2nd presidential debate from 1992 with Ross Perot, George Bush senior and Bill Clinton on* http://www.c-span.org/Watch/Media/1992/10/15/HP/A/10364/1992+Presidential+Town+Hall+Debate.aspx.

**1** *Note down your impressions of the candidates: how do they present themselves? Are they credible?*

**2** *Who would you vote for? Why?*

**3** *Check Carville's and Stephanopoulos's reactions after the debate. How do they react? Was the outcome of the debate successful for Bill Clinton?*


ISBN 978-3-12-577467-4

# Politics and Media – Your Opinion

**1** *To what extent has the film / have these films changed your attitude towards politics?*

**2** *Is the influence of the media dangerous for democratic elections?*




ISBN 978-3-12-577467-4

Klett

# Klausuren

# Klausur 1: Wag the Dog

*Watch the scene / read the screenplay to Brean's conversation with the CIA agent Young in chapter 9.*

Agent Young (to 2nd agent): … took you long enough.

2nd Agent Found 'em as soon as we could, sir.

Young After I'm done with 'em, what do you want me to do? Log them back to the District, or dump 'em out in the country, have the FBI trip over 'em?

2nd Agent Legal department says you pick 'em. Depends on what we want to do with them.

*Young walks over to Brean and Ames*

Young Two things I know to be true. There's no difference between good flan and bad flan. And there is no war. Guess who I am.

Ames I'd like to point out that I am under medical care and taking medication, the side-effects of which affected me a little…

Young Quite touching.

Ames (*stuttering*) And I also take this opportunity to suggest that, equally, I admit to nothing, and I would like my lawyer present.

Young (*nodding*) We show, and NSA confirms, there are no nuclear devices on the Canadian border. (*pause*) There are no nuclear devices in Albania. Albania has no nuclear capacity. Our spy satellites show no secret terrorist training camps in The Albanian Hinterland. The Border Patrol, the FBI, the R.C.M.P. report no, repeat: no untoward activity along our picturesque Canadian Border. The Albanian Government is screaming its defence, the world is listening. (*pause*) There is no war.

Brean (*gestures at the TV*) Of course there's a war. I'm watching it on television.

Young And who might you be, when it's all said and done?

Brean My name is Conrad Brean.

Young Who do you work for?

Brean Nobody whose name you want me to say, Mr. Young, I promise you.

Young It's all well and good, but when the fit hits the shan, somebody's going to have to stay after school, and who do you suppose that might be.

Brean I don't know what you're talking about.

Young The spy satellites show it, Mr. Brean, they show no war.

Brean Then what good are they, if they show no war, I mean what are we spending a quarter trillion dollars a year on the defence department, what good are they if they show nothing. What are they, are they useless or are they just broken, or what?

Ames And I'd like to point out that these medications taken in conjunction…

Brean If there's no threat then, where are you? When there's no threat what good are you?

Young Mr. Brean, you are the threat.


ISBN 978-3-12-577467-4

**Brean** I am the threat? I am the threat? Then what have I been doing the last 30 years that you haven't been doing. You wanna fill me in on that?

**Young** The last 30 years, Mr. Brean, I have been working to ensure the security of my country…

**Ames** As have we all….

**Brean** (*simultaneously with the above speech*): Well, I'm sure that speaks very well of you and for your parents. But if forced to choose between the security of the country and the security of your job, which would you pick. And, while you hesitate, permit me to suggest that they are one and the same. Your country and your job.

**Young** I'm doing my job, Mr. Brean. That's what you see me doing here. What is it you you're doing?

**Brean** I'm doing my job, too and let me ask you something, let me ask you a simple question: Why do people go to war? Why do they go to war?

**Young** I'll play your silly game.

**Brean** Why do they go to war?

**Young** To ensure their way of life.

**Brean** Would you go to war to do that?

**Young** I have.

**Brean** Well, if you went to war again, who would it be against? Your "ability to fight a two-ocean war" against who? Who? Sweden and Togo? That time is passed. It's over. The war of the future is nuclear terrorism. It is and it will be against a small group of dissidents who, unbeknownst, perhaps, to their own governments, have blah blah blah blah. And to go to that war, you have to be prepared. You got to be alert, and the public has to be alert. Because that is the war of the future, and if you're not gearing up, to fight that war, eventually the axe will fall. N'you're gonna be out in the street. And you can call this a "drill," or you can call it "job security," or you can call it anything you like. But I got one for you: you said, "Go to war to preserve your way of life," well, Chuck, this, this (*gestures around the room*) is your way of life. And if your spy satellites don't see nothing, if there ain't no war, then you can go home and prematurely take up golf, my friend, cause there ain't no war but ours.

*Ames looks at Young and smiles. They shake hands and afterwards Brean and Ames are free to go.*

*Transcript from* "Wag the Dog"

3 **District** Washington D.C. – 4 **FBI** the FBIs mission is to protect and defend the United States against terrorist and foreign intelligence threats, to uphold and enforce the criminal laws of the United States, and to provide leadership and criminal justice services to federal, state, municipal, and international agencies and partners. – 14 **NSA** the National Security Agency is a cryptologic intelligence agency of the United States government, administered as part of the United States Department of Defense. It is responsible for the collection and analysis of foreign communications and foreign signals intelligence. It is also responsible for protecting U.S. government communications and information systems from similar agencies elsewhere, which involves cryptography. – 17 **R. C. M. R.** Royal Canadian Mounted Police: the Canadian national police service and an agency of the Ministry of Public Safety Canada. – 25 **when the fit hits the shan** (when the shit hits the fan): when things go really bad really quickly and everybody in the vicinity is affected




ISBN 978-3-12-577467-4

## Tasks

**1 Comprehension**

*Sum up the scene in about 150 words.*

**2 Analysis**

*Characterize Brean and Ames and explain their individual reactions towards the CIA agent and analyse why it is possible that Brean convinces the CIA agent that there is a war. You may refer to other parts of the movie to support your arguments.*

**3 Comment**

**a)** *Comment either on Stanley Motss' statement in the very last chapter: "This is the best work I've ever done in my life because it's so honest." talking about his work for the president.*

OR

**b)** *Comment on the way the business of politics is characterized in the movie.*


ISBN 978-3-12-577467-4

# Klausur 2: Swing Vote

## Review of *Swing Vote* by Maitland McDonagh

Ostensibly a political satire with a heart of mush, Joshua Michael Stern hopelessly muddled film cries out for the firm hand of either a dyed-in-the-wool cynic like Billy Wilder, who would have put some teeth in its jabs at amoral politicians and blindly ambitious journalists. [...]

It's a presidential election year, and every-redneck Bud Johnson (Kevin Costner) couldn't care less: He lives in a trailer court in downtrodden Texico, New Mexico, works in an egg-packing factory and hasn't been sober since his wife decamped to become a C & W singer. Smart, resourceful, old beyond her years Molly Johnson (Madeline Carroll), who regularly picks up the slack for her useless father, optimistically exacts a promise that he'll exercise his civic responsibility by voting – she took the precaution of registering him by mail so he'd be eligible. Bud instead gets drunk, so Molly sneaks into Texico's lone polling station and surreptitiously casts a ballot on his behalf. Mechanical failure erases "Bud's" vote, but not the fact that it was cast, and the distribution of New Mexico's five precious electoral votes – and with them the outcome of a historically close election – suddenly come down to know-nothing Bud. As he waits to recast his vote in accordance with electoral law, both candidates – conservative Republican incumbent Andrew Boone (Kelsey Grammer) and liberal Democratic challenger Donald Greenleaf (Dennis Hopper) – swoop into Texico with their cynical campaign managers (Stanley Tucci, Nathan Lane), huge entourages and a small army of journalists determined to wring every possible career opportunity from the big carnival.

[...] the film's [...] fatal weakness is that it never successfully integrates two very different stories. Costner and Carroll have a touchingly bittersweet chemistry and Mare Winningham nails the role of drug-addicted runaway wife and mother Larissa in a single harrowing scene, but the Johnson family's dysfunctional dynamics are repeatedly shoved aside for wan political comedy. Both candidates are opportunists, who blithely abandon their supposed principles, but they're basically decent guys, and local ambitious journalist Kate Madison (Paula Patton) snatches her soul back from the devil at the 11th hour. The broad campaign-ad parodies make no sense – the candidates are wooing *Bud*, not the public, so why would they be spending money on TV commercials – and tiny Texico's dark night of the soul melts in the glare of klieg lights when the candidates finally come together for a gentlemanly one-on-one debate.

Satire should hurt and personal redemption needs to be earned; *Swing Vote* fails to deliver on both counts.



1 **ostensibly** supposedly – 1 **mush** soft mass – 1 **muddled** mixed-up – 2 **dyed-in-the-wool** eingefleischt, unverbesserlich – 2 **to put some teeth into sth** sich in einer Sache festbeißen – 3 **jab** punch – 4 **redneck** a white member of the Southern rural laboring class – 5 **trailer court** Wohnwagensiedlung – 5 **downtrodden** broken – 6 **to decamp** to run away, to flee – 6 **C & W** Country and Western – 7 **to pick up the slack** to do the work which someone else has stopped doing, but which still needs to be done – 8 **to exact** to demand – 10 **surreptitiously** secretly – 13 **incumbent** in office – 14 **swoop** jump, dive – 15 **entourage** group of attendants – 19 **harrowing** extremely agonizing and distressing – 19 **dysfunctional** abnormal – 20 **to shove aside** to push away – 20 **wan** *here:* weak, not of high quality – 21 **blithely** carelessly – 22 **to snatch her soul back from the devil in the 11th hour** decides to behave in a good and moral way just in time – 23 **to woo** to court, to flatter – 24 **glare** a fierce or angry stare – 25 **klieg light** a powerful carbon-arc lamp producing an intense light and used especially in making movies – 31 **redemption** salvation, rescue




ISBN 978-3-12-577467-4

## Tasks

### 1 Comprehension

*Sum up the author's opinion about the movie in no more than 150 words.*

### 2 Analysis

**a)** *There are film critics who call* Swing Vote *a satire, others say it's a comedy. Explain the difference between the two genres.*

**b)** *Give your own opinion about the genre of the movie supporting it with scenes or quotes from the movie.*

### 3 Comment

**a)** *Write a letter to McDonagh about her review of* Swing Vote *giving your own opinion about the movie.*

**b)** *Discuss this quote from another film critic about the message in* Swing Vote*:*

"Our political system doesn't encourage politicians to tell the truth, but to say what they think voters want to hear."


ISBN 978-3-12-577467-4

# Klausur 3

## Review of *The War Room* by Roger Ebert January 21, 1994

Professional campaign managers have had a bad image as long as they've had an image at all, [...]. The typical campaign manager is seen as a Machiavellian spin doctor, and that's on a good day.

Perhaps the documentary "The War Room" will bring a deeper dimension to the profession's image. At the very least, it may dispel the notion that campaign managers pervert the course of democracy with behind-the-scenes omniscience; the surprise in the film is that they're often as confused as their candidates sometimes seem to be.

[...], the movie follows key members of Bill Clinton's campaign team from the snows of New Hampshire in January, 1992, to the victory celebration in Little Rock in November of that year. The movie's stars are James ("The Ragin' Cajun") Carville, the impish chief strategist for the Clinton campaign, and George Stephanopoulos, the young, polished former Rhodes scholar who was the campaign's media director.

The two are seen working together in an inside-outside combination. Stephanopoulos, often in a suit and tie, handsome in a Kennedyesque way, is the relaxed, usually calm press spokesman. Carville, a tense and driven man who seems to shop for his clothes at the LSU sports store, works behind the scenes, often in the campaign's "war room" in a converted newspaper office in Little Rock.

Strategists would no doubt like to see themselves like modern Napoleons, moving pawns on the maps of continents. More often, this film shows, they get involved in screwy debates about the color, typography and size of their campaign posters. Their dedication to "the Candidate" is easily matched by the intensity with which they despise their opponents – and especially their opponents' troops, suspected in New Hampshire of tearing down Clinton signs (something, of course, Carville's volunteers would never, ever do . . . except, of course, in retaliation).

[...] Carville and Stephanopoulos [...] allow the cameras access to surprisingly unguarded moments, as when they brief their squad of spin doctors after one of the Clinton-Bush debates ("Just keep on repeating that Bush was on the defensive all night"), and when the press reports on Clinton's draft history, Carville complains, "Every time somebody even farts the word draft, it makes the paper." Given the various scandals and would-be scandals that pursued the Clinton campaign, it seems almost incredible that he survived, and won. There is footage from grim early days in New England, right after the supermarket tabloids broke the first charges of Clinton's adultery, and footage months later, two days before the election, of Stephanopoulos calmly talking on the phone with a man who had still more hearsay he wanted to ventilate. What you realize, watching Carville and Stephanopoulos move between grand strategy and damage control, is that they are good at their jobs, and probably as honest as was possible under the circumstances.

Carville is moving in a speech to his troops on the eve of the election. Exhausted, strung out, on the brink of tears, he tells them that politics has been his life, and that it is a life worth living. [...]



## Quotes from Roger Ebert's review of *Wag the Dog*, January 2, 1998

[...] Brean, [...], is a creature born to live in shadow, and De Niro plays him with the poker-faced plausibility of real spin doctors, who tell lies as a professional specialty. [...]

"Why does a dog wag its tail?" Brean asks at one point. ``Because the dog is smarter than the tail. If the tail was smarter, it would wag the dog." In the Breanian universe, the tail is smarter, and we, [...], are invited to be the dogs.

2 **Machiavellian** clever, devious, tricky – 4 **dispel** chase away – 5 **omniscience** state of possessing complete knowledge (Allwissenheit) – 9 **ragin'** (raging) furious, powerful, strong – 9 **Cajun** ethnic group mainly living in Louisiana, consisting of the descendants French-speaking settlers from the maritime provinces of what is now Canada – 9 **impish** naughty, mischievous – 10 **polished** elegant – 10 **Rhodes scholar** student who achieved the Rhodes Trust scholarship which enabled him to study him at Oxford University with financial support – 13 **Kennedyesque** like former US president John F. Kennedy – 14 **LSU** Louisiana State University – 15 **converted** changed, transformed – 16 **pawn** puppet – 17 **screwy** crazy – 18 **typography** lettering, print – 19 **to despise** to loathe, to hate – 21 **retaliation** revenge – 33 **tabloid** Klatschpresse, "Käseblatt" – 33 **adultery** disloyalty, betrayal (Ehebruch) – 35 **hearsay** rumour, word of mouth – 35 **to ventilate** to make know, to make public – 38 **eve** evening – 38 **to be strung out** to be tense, nervous – 41 **plausibility** credibility




ISBN 978-3-12-577467-4

## Tasks

**1 Comprehension**

*Sum up Roger Ebert's review of* The War Room *in no more than 150 words.*

**2 Analysis**

**a)** *Find possible reasons for the fact that Carville and Stephanopoulos let film-makers look into their work and explain them.*

**b)** *Do the quotes from* Wag the Dog *describe Carville's and Stephanopoulos' work well or are they beside the point?*

**3 Comment**

*Write your own review of either*

**a)** The War Room

OR

**b)** Wag the Dog.


ISBN 978-3-12-577467-4

# Lösungen

## Klausur 1

### 1 Comprehension

Brean and Ames are stopped on their way back to Washington by the CIA. They are taken to a restaurant where they are interviewed by CIA agent Young who found out about the fraud from the legal department who plans to have Ames and Brean arrested. Young quite arrogantly tells Ames and Brean right away that there is no war with Albania and that he can prove his allegation with pictures from spy satellites and other intelligence agencies. While Ames reacts shocked and tries to excuse her involvement in the affair with medication side effects, Brean stays calm and tells Young that the spy satellites are useless if they don't show a war. Leaving Ames completely out of the conversation Brean convinces Young with twisted arguments and clever phrasing that there is a war which needs the CIA's support. In the end Ames and Brean are free to go. (*149 words*)

### 2 Analysis

Ames is desperate and afraid. She believes that if the CIA has found out about the fraud everything will be over: her career and even her life. She blames Brean for this development and doesn't trust his spin doctor skills anymore. When agent Young sits down to talk to them she pretends to be under medical treatment taking a medication with side effects caused mental incapacity. She even behaves like a criminal wanting her lawyer present and refusing to answer any further questions. She interrupts the conversation twice with this explanantion and only stops when she feels that Brean is taking the lead in the interview. Her reaction shows how weak in character she really is. When she is trying to get back into the conversation twice it looks rather ridiculous because she is interrupted and then stopped by Brean, who is just more convincing and stronger with words than she is. She is not a manipulative and deceiving woman, she works hard for the president, constantly trying to be perfect, checking things twice before accepting them, like she does with Tracy's contract. She needs proof to accept things and to be confident about her actions. Because there is no real proof for a war in Albania – as the spy satellites claim – she loses all her confidence and relies on Brean to save her and the president from the CIA.

Brean behaves completely different. He's smiling confidently and ridicules Young's proves, telling him that the spy satellites must be broken and that they aren't any good and that the expenses for the defense department are useless if they are not spent on working spy "tools". He then tells him that if there wasn't any threat, Mr. Young would be out of work, geting even more beside the point, as it seems, but this is exactly the subject Brean wants to talk about with Young. With clever arguments and phrasing he gets Young to turn the conversation to his position in life and his job. Brean convinces him that Young has been to war for the last 30 years not only to ensure the security of the USA but also the security of his job and that this is the war that's going on at the moment. He turns Young around by telling him that the CIA has to prepare for a real war against nuclear terrorism in the future and if they don't, they'll be useless and out of a job. With strong arguments and a stream of many and fast spoken words Brean shuts Young up, he kills Young's arguments that there is no war. Brean never mentions a war with Albania; he only speaks of a war, meaning the war to preserve one's way of life with the re-election of the president. Due to Brean the atmosphere of the interview has changed in the end, Brean seems to have won over the CIA for his purposes; a war that cannot be seen by any spy satellite, but nevertheless is going on at the moment. The viewer will never find out why Young doesn't arrest Ames and Brean as planned, maybe because he believes Brean that the war is important enough to be pursued or merely because he doesn't want to lose his job. Brean tells Ames in the car that Young hadn't thought the whole thing through, a euphemism for turning him around 180 degrees. Brean is a spin doctor, he spins facts long enough the viewer, listener or reader doesn't know anymore what is true and what isn't. Brean doesn't lie or cheat all the time, he just puts facts together in a new combination the way he needs it. To support the impression that the great nation of the USA is willing to make peace with Albania, he lets the president accept a bundle of corn by an "Albanian" little girl and her grandmother, putting his coat around the grandmother's shoulders caringly when it starts to rain. When William Schumacher turns out to be a psychotic soldier, he turns his criminal past in to a post-war trauma that forces him to be on strong anti-psychotics. He finds a partner in Motss who not only has good ideas and can turn things around as skilfully as Brean, but who also doesn't have any scruples to manipulate the whole world for the purpose of the re-election of a president who has sexually molested a girl.

**3 Comment**

**a)** Individual answers. The students have to analyse in which way Motss uses the word "honest". He doesn't mean it in the sense of telling the truth because he created a fraud ("This is a complete fucking fraud and it looks 100% real", he says in the same scene) but in the sense of having created something praiseworthy. He is of the opinion that this "opus" is the most perfect thing he has ever produced. He fought off all odds and came to an ending that convinced the American public that much that the president is the perfect leader for their nation that they re-elected him. The phrase shows that he lacks the understanding that what he has done is unlawful. He has manipulated a complete nation, not only a movie audience. He has influenced world politics with his work, as the viewer finds out at the very end of the movie when it turns out that now there is a real attack from Albania. Motss hasn't done the job for the president as he claims but for himself, because he wants the credit as he continuously says in the last chapter. He even risks his life for this aim. In the end he dies without having achieved the credit, killed by his own vanity.

**b)** Individual answers. The students should mention that the business of politics is sometimes ruthless, unscrupulous and might even be immoral. To win or to achieve something is often more important than acting legally and for the good of the nation. The viewer doesn't know what good the president in *Wag the Dog* has achieved, he only knows that he molested a young girl. Such a kind of person doesn't seem appropriate in the position of a nation's leader. Still, with the help of Brean he is re-elected. The students should also elaborate on how the manipulation of the voter is shown in the movie and find own examples, e.g. Barack Obama behaving – or forced to behave – like a pop star in the election year of 2008, giving a speech in Berlin as part of his campaign. Examples from German elections are also possible. Finally, the students how dangerous it is to manipulate politics; as it turns out in the very last chapter of the movie when the new report attacks from an Albanian terrorist group. Of course, the viewer doesn't know whether this is real. The whole business of politics seems doubtful and the students should realize that criticism and doubts are not only good but seem necessary.

## Klausur 2

### 1 Comprehension

The author doesn't like the movie. In her opinion the film has neither a structure nor a message. She feels that the story about an underprivileged out-of-work single father becoming the most important person in the USA is not credible and not even funny. The real problems – Bud's alcohol abuse and the strange relationship with his daughter Molly – are less important than the funny scenes with the politicians. McDonagh finds the movie shallow and stereotypical: a nobody becomes a shining example of the possible change for the better everybody can go through. But Bud Johnson doesn't change because he wants to but because he has to for the sake of his daughter. His behaviour was inappropriate and made her run off to her mother. To get her back, he changed, not because he cared all of a sudden. The movie makes fun of important things without a real message, and McDonagh doesn't forgive this mistake.

### 2 Analysis

**a)** *Comedy* in film is a genre in which the main emphasis is on humour. Also, films in this style typically have a happy ending. Usually comedies are light-hearted stories with no intent other than to amuse.
Although *satire* is also meant to be funny, the purpose of satire is not primarily humour in itself so much as an attack on something of which the author strongly disapproves, using the weapon of wit.
In a comedy there is no criticism while a satire criticises not openly, but hidden in humour. While in comedies the humour is light-hearted and the plot is positive with a happy ending, the satire's humour is bitter-sweet and sometimes the laughter gets stuck in your throat.

**b)** Individual answers. The student's answer should use the definition given in **a** to explain their opinion about the genre of the movies and give at least three examples from the text supporting their opinion.

### 3 Comment

**a)** individual answers

**b)** Individual answers. Students should be able to realize that the statement is wrong. No democratic political system forces politicians to lie. A politician who lies to get votes will be unmasked quickly after the election and there will be ways he will be deposed from office. The statement is not the message of *Swing Vote* either. If there is a message at all it is that a person can change from an unimportant individual to the most important man of the country, the one to decide about the presidency. The movie is not about the president Boone and Mr. Greenleaf but about Bud Johnson. Not even Molly is important, even though she's much smarter than her father she is only a tool for Bud on his way to salvation – his own and that of the USA.

## Klausur 3

### 1 Comprehension

Roger Ebert sees the documentary *The War Room* as a breakthrough in investigative journalism. Through this movie, Americans are given the possibility to understand the ways a campaign is run. The campaign managers are no longer manipulative, cold-blooded spin doctors, but men who simply do their jobs: meet the press, spread the good news and protect their candidate. The job as a campaign manager isn't a glamorous one with life in hotel suites and expensive dinners but a life in a relatively small office – the war room – with too little space for all the workers. The phone is ringing constantly, there is always bad news to be dealt with and the only positive events are the debates – if they are won. In Ebert's eyes the main actors of the movie, Carville and Stephanopoulos, laid the basis for an honest style of politics by giving an insight in their work. (149 words)

### 2 Analysis

**a)** Individual answers. The students should realize though that the movie was a great opportunity for both Carville and Stephanopoulos to become famous or known to the people after the campaign. Without the movie they probably would have sunk into oblivion after Clinton was elected for president. Their willingness to give film makers an insight in their work shows their self-confidence and courage. They definitely had something to say about what would be shown in the movie and what would be cut but still there are moments in the documentary when they look tired and anxious because things are not going well for Clinton at all.
In *Swing Vote* Greenleaf's campaign manager says that the campaigns you lose are of no importance because the voters forget them quickly. Students could mention either this or give examples themselves from the present. Not only campaign managers are forgotten quickly but also the candidates: who still remembers Ross Perot, Paul Dukakis, Ralph Nader or even John McCain? They vanished into oblivion shortly after the elections.

**b)** Of course Brean is not the president's official campaign manager, but he too runs a campaign which might be of even greater importance. He tries to save the president's re-election. The president has to be saved from prosecution; this asks for a greater event that catches the public's eye. Clinton's affairs with other women are not a crime but merely a dark spot in the candidate's reputation.
Carville and Stephanopoulos use the same strategy as Brean does: they distract the public. They focus on Bush's broken promises and on political issues rather than private problems. Here the scene with the news about campaign posters being printed in Brazil is important. The campaign managers try to draw the public eye to Bush's broken promise of creating new jobs in the USA. Their effort fails but still this is the same method Brean uses. Carville and Stephanopoulos want the voters to see that Clinton is a better president that Bush is, no matter whether he cheated on his wife or not. They bend the truth a bit and interpret events differently so the voter might change his mind. And that is the exact same thing Brean does, even though he takes thing farther by inventing a war, a war hero and

a burial of a war hero. Brean is the tail which wags the dog, namely the voters, while Carville and Stephanopoulos are more of a head that leads the dog/ voters in the direction they want.

**3 Comment**

Individual answers for both **a)** and **b)**. The students should realize the style of a review from Ebert's example: "catchy" introduction, description of the most important events of the plot and one's personal opinion either already in the introduction or the closing paragraph. Concerning *The War Room* the special techniques and the difference between a documentary and a movie should be mentioned, as for *Wag the Dog* the genre of satire needs to be explained.

# Literatur

# Literaturliste


## Literatur

Becker, Horst u. a.: Leitfragen Politik. Orientierungswissen politische Bildung. Stuttgart: Klett, 2003, S. 301 ff.

Beckmann-Schulz, Petra: Präsidentschaftswahlen in den USA. Bundeszentrale für politische Bildung: Themenblätter für den Unterricht, Nr. 36. Bonn: Franzis, 2004.

Lösche, Peter und Hartmut Wasser: Politisches System der USA. Informationen zur politischen Bildung Nr. 283. Bonn: Franzis 2004.

Tindall, George Brown und David E. Shi: America. A Narrative History. Norton & Company, 7th edition, 2007, Volumes 1 & 2.

Anonymous: Primary Colors: A Novel of Politics. Random House: 1996


## DVDs / Filme

The Candidate (UK 1998): Robert Redford plays an idealistic senate candidate Bill McKay. He's mainly running to bring certain political issues into the broad public, although he never actually plans to win. But he must realize that whether or not he wins, he might not be able to hold on to his values.

Primary Colours (USA 1998): John Travolta stars as the exuberant, larger-than-life, shrewd and sentimental presidential candidate, Jack Stanton, a man with oversized appetites for almost everything. Also stars Emma Thompson, Billy Bob Thornton and the excellent Kathy Bates.

Zusatzmaterial zu vielen Filmen: Trailer, Interviews, Biographien der Schauspieler und Regisseure…

## Internetadressen

Internet Movie Data Base: http://www.imdb.com

Parteien:

www.gop.com (Internetseite der Republikanischen Partei der USA)

www.democrats.org (Internetseite der Demokratischen Partei der USA)

## Allgemeine Recherche und Online-Nachschlagewerke

www.bpb.de (Bundeszentrale für politische Bildung, Materialien für den Unterricht – leider auf Deutsch – vielfältig als PDF-Datei herunterzuladen. Themenhefte und die Informationen zur politischen Bildung können dort kostengünstig online bestellt werden. )

www.wikipedia.org (Online-Enzyklopädie, die sicherlich kritisch betrachtet und benutzt werden muss, deren Qualität sich jedoch stark verbessert hat und die sehr hilfreich sein kann.)

www.britannica.com (Online-Version der Encyclopedia Britannica. Ergebnisse klar gegliedert, Nachschlagen von Wortbedeutungen möglich, ebenso wie die Benutzung des Thesaurus, leider muss man sich für manche Funktionen anmelden)

http://encyclopedia.thefreedictionary.com (sehr ausführliche Online-Enzyklopädie, alle Ergebnisse frei verfügbar).

http://www.gwu.edu/~action/P2008.html („Democracy in Action", Projekt der George-Washington-Universität, Fachbereich „political communication" mit dem Fokus auf die Analyse von audiovisuellen Medien in den Präsidentschaftswahlkampagnen)

http://www.techpresident.com/ (Internetseite, die sich mit dem Internet als neues Wahlmedium bzw. als neuer Wahlplattform beschäftigt. Untersucht wird, wie häufig die Kandidaten das Internet nutzen und ebenso, wie die Wähler dieses neue Medium einsetzen.)

## Material für Hörverstehensübungen

http://www.youthradio.org/election2008/

http://www.npr.org

http://www.americanrhetoric.com/speechbank.htm